GUIDE COLLOMB

6. VANOISE PARK

TARENTAISE & HAUTE MAURIENNE

D1512783

Gde. Casse summit ridge

AIG. DE LA
VANOISE

VANOISE PARK

TARENTAISE & HAUTE MAURIENNE

Mountain walking, scrambling and trail guide
with selected principal ascents and standard mountain climbs

ROBIN G. COLLOMB

West Col

VANOISE PARK

First published in Britain 1988 by
West Col Productions
Goring   Reading   Berks.   RG8 9AA

SBN   906227 37 2

Diagrams by Stephanie Collomb
Photographs West Col Archives

Printed in England by Swindon Press Ltd
Swindon   Wilts.

Contents

Illustrations

• Key to huts and other mountain bases shown on map overleaf.

1	Mt. Pourri / Regaud	R.41,42
2	Rosuel	R.23,40
3	La Martin	R.45
3A	Turia	R.44 (E of Aig. Rouge)
4	Plaisance	R.49
5	Col du Palet	R.46,47,48
5A	Laisonnay	R.51
5B	Bois	R.52
6	Plan des Gouilles	R.53,54
7	Grand Bec	R.59,60,61
8	Col de la Vanoise	R.57,58,64,81
9	Leisse	R.65,66,67
10	Fond des Fours	R.70
11	Lacs Merlet	R.56
11A	Saut	R.55
12	Vallette	R.73,74
13	Entre Deux Eaux	R.63,64
14	Femma	R.68,69
15	Péclet-Polset	R.71
16	Génépy	R.72
17	Arpont	R.79,80,81,82,83,84
18	Mollard	R.87
19	Plan du Lac	R.33,62
20	Vallonbrun	R.86
21	Fond Aussois	R.76,77
22	Dent Parrachée	R.78
23	Plan Sec	R.78a
24	Orgère	R.14,36,75
25	Cuchet	R.85
26	Ruitor	R.88
27	La Motte	R.89
28	Le Saut	R.90
29	Prariond	R.91
30	Carro	R.92,93
31	Evettes	R.94
32	Gastaldi	R.207, 209 preamble
33	Avérole	R.95
34	Arcelle Neuve	R.97

ABBREVIATIONS

Aig.	Aiguille	Ital.	Italian
biv.	bivouac	km	kilometres
Br.	Brèche (gap)	L	left (direction)
br.	bridge	M	map scale, representing
c.	circa, approximately		1000, eg. 50M = 1/50,000
CAF	French Alpine Club	m	metres
CAI	Italian Alpine Club	min.	minutes
Cent.	Central	Mt.	Mont
ch.	chalet(s)	N	north
Dt.	Dent	n.	number
E	east	PNV	Vanoise National Park
EDF	State Electricity Board	pt.	spot height, or position on a route
Fr.	French	Pte.	Pointe
Gd(e).	Grand(e)	R	right (direction)
gl.	glacier	R.	route number (cross ref.)
GR	Grande Randonnée	S	south
GTA	Bunkhouse Touring Association	sta.	station
		TCF	French Touring Club
h	hour(s)	TCI	Italian Touring Club
IGM	Italian Government Map	var.	variation/variant
		W	west
IGN	French Government Map		

Intermediate compass directions are indicated: SW, NE, etc.

Grading of technical climbs

Overall and numerical rock climbing equivalents, approximately translated into English as follows: Easy/Moderate, Moderately Difficult, Fairly Difficult, Difficult, Very Difficult, Extremely Difficult, and Exceptionally Difficult = F (I), PD (II), AD (III), D (IV), TD (V), ED (VI), XD (VII). Minus and plus signs are added to denote respectively lower and upper limits within particular grades. Parts of climbs graded for using artificial aids are indicated for degree/extent/difficulty in rising order: A1, A2, A3, A4.

Nearly all walks, trails and scrambles described in this guide have no technical grading. Where a route may occasionally involve the application of proper mountaineering techniques, this is specified and where necessary graded accordingly.

MAPS

1/250,000	IGN	Red series n.112 Savoie Dauphiné
1/100,000	IGN	Green series n.53 Grenoble–Mont Blanc
1/50,000	DR/IGN	composite series n.11 Vanoise National Park
1/50,000	IGN	statutory coverage: Orange series –

3532 Bourg St. Maurice	3632 Ste. Foy Tarentaise
3533 Moûtiers	3633 Tignes
3534 Modane	3634 Lanslebourg

1/25,000   IGN Violet tourist series. Withdrawn in 1986 with no equivalent replacements. Set of 3 called Massif de la Vanoise – n.235 Tarentaise, n.236 Grande Casse – Dent Parrachée, n.237 Haute Maurienne

1/25,000   Double Blue series, equivalent to statutory coverage, with tourist information overprinted where a purple dot appears on front of map. Some of these maps overlap slightly, and others border areas where the regular blue series (2 over the area of each 1/50,000 map) commences.

3532E Bourg St. Maurice	3632W Ste. Foy Tarentaise
3533W Moûtiers Plagne	3633E Val d'Isère
Courchevel	3634W Lanslebourg Mont Cenis
3533E Tignes Pralognan	3634E Bessans Pte. de
3534W Modane	Charbonnel

Appropriate maps in this series are cited for all important route descriptions in the guide.

1/25,000   DR/IGN ski area series n.18 Les Trois Vallées

All maps are stocked by and available from West Col Productions.

OFFICIAL FRENCH LONG DISTANCE TRAIL GUIDES – CNSGR

In the Grande Randonnée series one volume covers GR 5 – 55 and variants from N to S across the Vanoise park area: Section – Croix du Bonhomme à Modane. Guides in this series are being progressively reformated and also made available in English.

Gîte d'étape – bunkhouse; owners are often members of the national GTA association; very good simple, cheap accommodation, with self catering or meals provided as a simple restaurant service. Usually located in valleys and plainly marked on 50M and 25M maps.

Introductory

Inaugurated in 1963 as the first Alpine region in France to be set aside for preservation, the Vanoise Park takes its name from the twin features of a high trough situated roughly in the centre of the region and an associated huge snow blanket – the second largest icecap of its kind in the Alps – spreading S from the Col de la Vanoise. In fact the term Vanoise emanates from a native description of furious blasts of wind sweeping the broad trough of the pass – the crossing of which in stormy conditions was much feared by the inhabitants of Pralognan and Termignon in the 17th and 18th centuries.

Within limits defined by a circular valley system comprised of the Isère, the Arc and their tributaries, the oval shaped park boundaries so drawn correspond to the ground described by the older regional Roman name of Tarentaise. Only the southern fringe, rising as a wall above the deep Arc valley, belongs to the neighbouring district called Haute Maurienne. Both are part of the province of Savoie.

The original Roman name for these mountains is Graian Alps. In topographical order the Vanoise/Tarentaise portion represents the Western Graians, ie. the massif situated entirely in France. The frontier ridge with Italy hems in the eastern and southern flanks of the Isère and the Arc to form the Central Graians, while further E another massif of similar dimensions is revealed in Italy as the Gran Paradiso, or Eastern Graians, a national park since 1922-25.

In reality the park zone occupies barely half the area of the Tarentaise and Haute Maurienne. The rest is encompassed by an outer boundary described as a "peripheral" zone in which the statutory park regulations do not apply. The only explanation for this curious definition of inner and outer zones is that winter sports developers, the state electricity authority, and others had already gained a strong foothold in many of the important access valleys, where their advancement continues unchecked. These encroachments come right up to the foot of the highest peaks, so that the inner boundary is drawn with many tortuous twists and indentations. Some examples include the boundary laid along crests of the Péclet-Polset group; a corner only 250m below the top of the Gde Motte; another corner touching the summits of the Dôme de la Sache and Mt Turia – consequently verging on the apex of Mt Pourri. Owing to the unsatiated resort expansion at La Plagne, the fine Sommet de Bellecôte is excluded from the park altogether.

These contradictions of the park concept can be set against some bene-
fits resulting from the creation of the peripheral zone; it extends well
beyond the Tarentaise to embrace the Haute Maurienne slope of the
Central Graian frontier ridge - a sensible annexation along the full
length of the ridge from the Petit St Bernard pass in the N to Modane
in the S. Little change has taken place in this huge boomerang shaped
slot of ground in the last 25 years. Restraints have been imposed with
some success - notably in access valleys where cars could once go but
are now banned (Ribon, Avérole, Ecot, Sassière, etc.).

The British were among the first travellers to be attracted to this area.
Within a short period during the 19th century a considerable achieve-
ment is recorded in their tourist ascents of all the major peaks without
exception in the Tarentaise, and of all but 4 on the Central Graians
ridge. The quaint and quiet atmosphere of the region reported by the
English in books and articles right up to the 1950s hardly seems belie-
vable today, so great are the changes wrought on this mountainscape.

Returning to the beginning, J.T. Needham and 2 other Englishmen
made a bold crossing of the Tarentaise in 1751 from Bourg St Maurice
to Termignon via Peisey Nancroix (then with a silver mine worked by
English owners), Col de la Tourne, Col de la Leisse, Entre-deux-Eaux
and the Plan du Lac. In 1829 the first detailed descriptions of the area
were given by William Brockedon. Of Val d'Isère he wrote: "... the
spire of the highest church-village appeared surrounded by a few houses.
What was called the auberge was a filthy miserable den; but there was
readiness to oblige, and a zeal in my service which reconciled me to
the privations it threatened".

Brockedon crossed the Col de la Vanoise and noted "enormous glaciers
and inaccessible peaks". Pralognan in 1834 was situated "in beautiful
meadows and calm retirement of the valley ... on entering the village
a narrow lane ... leads to the only inn ... miserable accommodation
can only be obtained."

☐   ☐   ☐   ☐

Recent developments for tourism and outdoor activities amount to some
of the most prominent examples of environmental desecration perpetrated
anywhere in the Alps. The park has had to be squeezed into the hither-
to untouched high ground - a genuine wilderness area now hopefully to
be preserved in its natural state. But the credo of easy access and min-
imum inconvenience for the public to pursue all kinds of leisure pursuits
is supported by the stepping-stone of the commercialised peripheral zone
and by a new chain system of huts constructed in the central park area
itself. It will be argued that a foremost object and attraction of a park
is to facilitate access, but this notion cannot escape a consequential
urbanisation and reduction in the quality of the mountain experience.

At one end of the spectrum massed armies of skiers are now able to indulge in their downhill only sensations all year round. Mechanical lifts reach to well over 3000m in a series of criss-cross chessboard moves across rows of valleys and ridges. This gigantic sprawl of pylons and cables has overwhelmed a quarter of the Tarentaise. On the grounds of safety, an exclusiveness has been awarded to some of these lifts so that they are reserved for skiers - pedestrians are barred. Worse still, some pistes descend snowfields and glaciers previously ascended by climbers who in turn are now forbidden to tread this terrain.

At the opposite extreme are long caterpillars of a new breed of walker, called backpackers. Before the park was established mountain walking in mainly remote valleys and over empty grassy passes was a pastime followed generally by alpinists moving between centres of climbing interest. A handful of CAF or small private huts served the region, and often there was no overnight shelter for some expeditions; you camped or bivouacked. Now the PNV has built, or has converted from tumbled down chalets, about 20 new huts, most of them in a comparatively lavish style as regards comfort and amenities. You enjoy unprecedented elbow and leg room, like first-class air travel, compared with the sprinkling of traditional or climbers' huts, always remembered for their spartan furnishings and cramped quarters. Walkers can backpack anywhere and find comfortable lodgings rarely more than 5h distance from the last overnight halt.

GR long distance trails n.5, 55 and their variations weave across the region from N to S and are waymarked as clearly as city streets - as are shorter walking circuits, known as balcony trails, and nature trails, which have been mapped out round snowy massifs and along the sides of valleys between the floor and the snowline, some of only 1 or 2h.

The lowest common denominator is expressed to the invading hordes as the right to enjoy the heritage of a mountain landscape girt with forests, pastures and varied plants, populated with several animal species and birds, rivers stocked with fish, and the total scenic grandeur measured by its many rock types and forms.

Special interest and activity groups are still the minority worldwide in visits to national parks. The trend in current publicity for the Vanoise is to convert everyone from the immobile and aimless beach mentality indulged in at roadhead carparks to getting out and stretching their legs uphill. Scores of noticeboards have been erected to explain the "rules and regulations" for public behaviour in the park. New controls have become necessary as the number of visitors grows. Camping, for instance, is restricted to approved sites. While most of these are excellent there are still many valley bases where camping is not permitted. Wild camping is forbidden, especially at hut sites - as was practised in the past above the treeline and up to the snow line. Some relaxation of this rule is becoming evident, especially in the peripheral zone. Serious overcrowding in huts has forced the authorities to ignore infringements. Close supervision of these and many other matters is carried out by teams of field wardens; they come down heavily on flower-pickers (unless licensed) and people with dogs off a lead (strictly speaking domestic pets are forbidden in the park area proper).

The unstoppable upsurge of ski resorts changes the Vanoise map annually. The Trois Vallées area claims to be the world's biggest ski playground. However, Val d'Isère is the most celebrated. It was the first to be developed as an integrated centre (1948) and now seems the least obtrusive. No notable new skyscrapers or extensions in apartment blocks have gone up for some years. Ski tows shoot up in more directions but they are dormant in summer. The new, all-year-round Fornet-Col de l'Iseran cableway has raised some eyebrows. Its purpose is to take summer skiers from Val d'Isère to the col without using private transport, or waiting for infrequent buses along the road to the col. At the top a surfaced lane extends to skitows on the Gd. Pisaillas gl. under the Pers-Montet ridge. Below Val d'Isère the Daille lift system has been supplemented with a partly underground funicular capable of transporting some 3000 people an hour to the slopes behind the Bellevarde.

In the Trois Vallées area Méribel and Courchevel remain minor monstrosities when set against the undertakings to satisfy the appetite of skiers in the third and until recently most unspoiled centre now called Val Thorens. The long-promised developments have begun in earnest. Condominium buildings of great size and ugliness have sprung up over the bare mountainside. The tentacles of cableways, chairlifts and tows of astonishing density extend in all directions to the surrounding heights. From Les Menuires (known in the trade as Les Manures) on the E side of the valley mountain transport reaches the ridge dividing it from Méribel at the Trois Marches station, and from here there are cableway connections NE joining all the Trois Vallées ski stations in turn across the Saulire summit. This interweaving of the valleys spawns a 400 km network of marked runs among 160 lifts.

While Méribel and Courchevel have become acceptable summer eyesores, appealing gradually to more of the ski-less summer trade, Val Thorens belongs to another category of exploitation. At its head lies the permanently snow covered Péclet-Polset massif where the dual objective is to make skiing possible all year round. 2 lifts already attain the crest zone of the massif, and so provide runs on the Péclet, Thorens and Chavière gls. For the lame or lazy climber this previously rarely visited valley with its long remembered walk-up now becomes the easiest and shortest way to reach the chief summits of the massif.

Other newly created ski resorts lie on the N slope of the park above the Middle Isère. Among these La Plagne is the most grandiose, filling 2 large grassy hollows above a vast belt of forest. The dominant landmarks are buildings the size of battleships, housing the complete services of a town like the inside of a department store. You need a corridor and alley plan to find a way through the maze. The Rochette cableway at La Plagne attains a ridge from which, despite its modest elevation, offers expressly the best view of the Vanoise park to be obtained from any restaurant platform in the region. Then the longest cableway, of 6.5km, in the Tarentaise has been constructed here, reaching the Chiaupe gl. on the W side of the Bellecôte summit. Previously quite remote and little visited this mountain with its exceptional panorama can now be climbed easily from the top station in $1\frac{1}{2}$ h.

Above Bourg St. Maurice the latest sacrifice to winter worshippers awaits the bricks and steel approach to progress. Les Arcs was begun, like many before it, in altitude stages; Arc 1600, Arc 1800 and Arc 2000. The last, though basically completed, looks set for a massive expansion. Just how far this centre will probe the Mt. Pourri massif remains to be seen; its radial glaciers are much steeper than the Péclet and Bellecôte, and normally badly crevassed.

The last word on this subject must address Tignes and the Grande Motte, where foul deeds have been committed. Virtually separate from Val d' Isère, though linked unnecessarily across a dividing ridge by uphill transport, a good road connection goes round the bottom to reascend to the Lac de Tignes site where one of the least harmonious and hideous resort constructions in the Alps is found. An architectural disaster, many of the buildings already look like urban slums. The prevailing impression is one of being stranded in the isolation that can be felt in a small run-down township of the American West. The main cableway here stretches in 2 stages to 3440m on the NE ridge of the Grande Motte. In good conditions the summit can be reached in under 1 h, compared with 6h at least before the cableway was built. Almost without precedent in the Alps on a mountain of this stature relative to its area, the Grande Motte has had to acquire an entirely new and previously rarely done normal route for climbers wishing to enjoy an ascent untrammelled by sight or sound of the cableway and its glacier teeming with skiers.

Pralognan, the most traditional and agreeable summer resort, nicely situated in the centre of the park, is ignored by package tour skiers. The accessible winter slopes are either of modest length, or grade IV. Besides, it hardly sees the winter sun. None of the projects named in in the 1950s, to join Pralognan to the Chasseforêt-Vanoise snowfield, and in the opposite direction to link hands with Courchevel over the Gde. Pierre pass, have come to fruition – and must presumably remain so.

Approaches by public transport

From Paris by rail to Moûtiers or Bourg St. Maurice (N side); or to Modane (S side); frequent trains in summer. Geneva is the nearest convenient international airport for the N side; Geneva – by road/bus – via Annecy, Ugine, Albertville – to Moûtiers, 110 km. New motway projected. Turin airport is closer to S side; from here by train to Modane, 90 km, or by bus via Susa and over the Montcenis to the Arc valley and Lanslebourg, 80 km. Shorter through the Fréjus tunnel but expensive.

Peripheral valley system and transport

This consists of the Isère (N and NE) and Arc (SE and S), the 2 divided by the Col de l'Iseran. Good motor road throughout with some parts normally under repair every year. Between Bourg St. Maurice and Val d'Isère, some narrow stretches and several tunnel/gallery sections. The col with many sharp bends is closed on both sides in winter; normally open June to October; 2 buses daily in summer cross it from Val d'Isère to Bonneval-sur-Arc; laybys and parking on several bends, easier on the Isère (N) side. The Arc road is fast down to Lanslebourg then more twisting and slower to Modane.

Frequent buses: Albertville – Moûtiers – Bourg St. Maurice, also served by railway. Then about 4 buses daily Bourg St. Maurice – Val d' Isère. Modane – Termignon – Lanslebourg, then about 3 buses daily Lanslebourg – Bessans – Bonneval.

Access valleys and transport

Summer buses; all good metalled roads.

1 Moûtiers – Pralognan, 28 km. 5 times daily, more frequent as far as Bozel, 13 km.

2 Moûtiers – Val Thorens, 35 km. Twice daily.

3 Moûtiers – Méribel, 17 km. 3 times daily.

4 Moûtiers – Courchevel, 24 km. 3 times daily

5 Moûtiers – Bozel (Pralognan road), then minibus to Champagny, 19 km. Twice daily. Taxis and cars can continue by rough road to Laisonnay d'en haut, 8 km.

6 Moûtiers – La Plagne, 33 km. Twice daily. Or from Bourg St. Maurice, 28 km. Sideroad to Plagne-Bellecôte, 3 km, by minibus, unsurfaced continuation to Les Arpettes.
Railway in main Isère valley, Moûtiers – Bourg St. Maurice, with

halts at Aime (for La Plagne) and Landry (for Nancroix).

7 Moûtiers – Peisey Nancroix, changing at Landry, 33km. 3 times daily. Or from Bourg St. Maurice direct, via Landry, 14km, about 3 times. Continuation road to Porte de Rosuel, minibus, 5km.

8 Bourg St. Maurice – Arc Pierre Blanche 1600, 17km, twice daily; cableway alternative; road continues to Arc 2000, taxi hire, 11km (eventually, bus service).

9 Bourg St. Maurice – Lac de Tignes, 31km, combined with Val d' Isère service, 3-4 times daily. Val d'Isère-Lac de Tignes (13km), in Aug.-Sept. only (or private minibus hire).

10 Bonneval – l'Ecot roadhead, 4 km. Sometimes open/sometimes closed to cars; otherwise taxis permitted.

11 Bessans – Avérole roadhead, 7km. Closed to cars beyond pt. 1802 (traffic island); taxis are allowed to go beyond this point.

11a Bessans – Ribon valley; closed to all except official 4WD.

12 Termignon – Bellecombe roadhead, 12km, private minibus or taxi, easy for cars, large carpark.

13 Modane – Aussois, 9 km, twice weekly (!). Taxi hire. Continuation road to Plan d'Amont barrage, 6km, taxi hire, large carpark.

14 Modane – Porte de l'Orgère, 14km, private minibus or taxi, car parking area.

Other roads passable for cars to approved roadhead parking are included in appropriate route descriptions.

VALLEY BASES

Moûtiers   510m

15 Middle Isère spa resort, all main services, popular summer touring centre, bus and railway stations. Traffic diversions and complicated vehicle circulation. All classes of hotels and lodgings. In a hanging valley 20 km W of Moûtiers lies the small, purpose-built Valmorel resort (1400m); road link across a ridge W to the Col de la Madeleine road border of the Tarentaise.

Pralognan   1418m

16 See R.1. Famous, historical village, originally populated by Swiss migrants, picturesque and pleasant to the eye, senior park resort. All main services, supermarkets, tourist office, alpine museum, guides'

bureau, 30 hotels/inns; apartments; no petrol station (last fill-up at Brides-les-Bains, 6km this side of Moûtiers). Surreptitious bunkhouse accommodation; inquire at tourist office; also 24 bunkhouse places at campsite (see below). At least 3 premises claim gîte d'étape service.

A river bridge divides the village into 2 parts; easier parking before this. At back of resort huge campsite dispersed in 3 directions; access through one-way system of lanes at top of main street after bridge. Car drivers approaching the campsite should take a fork R (straight on for bridge) and bypass built up area to a sharp turn L between fields. Go down here to 1st turning R, leading in a short distance to the main site entrance on L; arrivals office, h.& c. running water, all mod. cons. At top of main street, cableway to Mt. Bochor (2023m). Small road to les Fontanettes (1644m) and Pont de l'Eau (1676m), carparking, for Cirque de l'Arcelin walks.

The main valley road continues S for 6km to large parking area beside the Doron de Chavière river – just before the Pont de la Pêche (1764m). Starting point for numerous walks and expeditions.

Val Thorens   2325/2350m

17   See R.2.   The roadhead in the Belleville valley (no petrol after Moûtiers) remains to be determined.   At present a broad rough highway abuts a chaotic parking area in several slanting levels between huge apartment blocks and smaller hotels, shops and restaurants (limited food purchase).   Tennis courts, swimming pool and other amusements.   The cheapest accommodation for walkers/climbers is at the likeable solitary refuge called Chalet Caron at a bend in the last part of the road at pt. 2197; unmade lane access from here.   Bunkhouse with mattresses, mod. cons, simple restaurant service.   From Val Thorens centre, cableways and chairlifts operate in summer to the Mont de Péclet (no problems), Péclet gl. (separate ticket and charges for 'pedestrians' who may be turned away if operators consider the gl. to be 'dangerous'; brandish an ice axe and crampons), Col de Thorens (similar problems, but as this is a 2-stage chairlift the ticket office is less vigilant).   Other lifts reserved for winter and spring may open during the summer.   When conditions become too icy for skiing (often from early Aug.) all lifts may be closed.   Note, there is no campsite at Val Thorens, and campers are chased off.

Méribel-les-Allues   1500/1680m

18   See R.3.   The road to this celebrated skiing complex latterly rises above the valley floor to reach the main centre on a W-facing slope with rows of buildings in arcades interwoven by zigzags.   All main services, many hotels and assorted bunkhouse accommodation for summer

visitors. No official camping. Main cableway system rises to the Saulire summit, where another descends to Courchevel. The valley road
continues for 4km to Méribel-Mottaret (1681m), minibus service and
cableways to the Saulire and to the ridge (road to 1793m) boundary
with Val Thorens.

Courchevel 1757m

19 See R.4. Called Courchevel 1850. The main resort lies on the
westward of 2 parallel N-S ridges, so that Courchevel 1650 (1564m)
is perched on the E side ridge, and Courchevel 1550 (1479m) near the
valley bed between them. A network of small roads extends S; some
of them are banned to motorists. Cableway to the Saulire connects
directly with Méribel. The Ariondaz lift (Mont Bel-Air) and associated chairlifts are the most useful for reaching good walking country.
Comprehensive amenities and services, including swimming pools, tennis courts, alpine garden, etc. Many hotels and apartments, bunkhouse
accommodation; no official campsite. Note: the original and proper
name of Courchevel 1650 = Moriond.

Champagny 1200/1250m

20 See R.5. String of pretty hamlets at entrance to valley of same
name. A few small hotels/inns, and shops. No official camping; the
approved site is situated 4km further up the road E, just before Champagny-le-Haut (1470m); PNV hut here, and higher up another private
hut at Laisonnay d'en Haut (1575m). Narrow motor road, Champagny
to Laisonnay (taxi hire). See R.51,52.

La Plagne 1976m

21 See R.6. A plantation of tower blocks. This lofty ski resort is
being extended by roads to outlying purpose-built 'villages'. In the
summer all services operate; modest hotel terms are difficult to find.
Cableway to the Grande Rochette; magnificent view of the Vanoise
park. At pt.1886 on approach road, turning L(E) to Plagne Bellecôte (1900m), one-way circular road access system. High-rise flats,
apartments and shops; tennis, swimming, etc.; no camping, crowded
carparking. All open in summer to serve the 6.5km Mio-Bellecôte
cableway for skiing on the Chiaupe gl. Nearest petrol station is at
Aime on the Moûtiers-Bourg St. Maurice road.

Landry 778m

22 See R.7. Small, quiet village at entrance to Ponturin valley for
Peisey Nancroix. One hotel, one inn, separate resturant, bars, good
foodstore beside church. Behind church, small campsite at top of apple

orchard; mod. cons, h. & c. water. Another campsite on Peisey road nearly one km outside village has no services and is abysmal. For exploring walks and climbs on N side of park, easily the best valley base for those with a car.

Peisey Nancroix   1298/1312m

23   See R.7.   Ponturin valley.   Simple village centre with 2 hotels, inns and small shops in a valley where most summer visitor practise the art of comfortable camping.   Road access to Plan Peisey and Les Arcs resorts.   At the next hamlet, Moulin (1 km), similar amenties; next at Nancroix hamlet (1438m), the same; supermarket here at sharp bend in road.   Soon after this the official campsites commence on R(S) side of road, straggling for one km along meadow and forest, access lanes and parallel backroad; all mod. cons.   The last hamlet is les Lanches (1523m) and the road continues to huge carpark on L side at the Porte de Rosuel (1556m).   PNV hut, restaurant, etc.   Premier N entrance to park.   Nearest petrol station, Bourg St. Maurice.

Les Arcs   1600/2000m

24   See R.8.   Arc Pierre Blanche (1600m) has basic accommodation and services in summer.   The access road from Bourg St. Maurice starts from main road near Séez village, altogether 17 km.   A cableway is much quicker (3 km).   Road continuation to Arc 2000 where summer facilities are also very basic (11 km).   Splendid, remote location now criss-crossed with skitows.   Roadhead and parking under huge grotesquely ugly building on N side of Lac des Combes.   Continuation to the Arc chalet refuge (qv).

Bourg St. Maurice   813m

25   Modest small town resort and railhead near bend marking division between the Middle and Upper Isère.   The centre is bypassed by main road (railway station), comprehensive services.   Cableway to Arc 1600.

Les Brevières   1559m   Tignes   1797m

26   See R.9.   Below and adjoining the Tignes Barrage in the Isère valley.   Numerous small hotels, pensions, main services.   Camping on a knoll between the 2 villages.   A better location in summer than the Lac de Tignes.   Local bus uses the old riverbed road below main Isère highway; transporter cablelift.

Lac de Tignes / Val Claret   2093/2127m

27   See R.9.   Considerable publicity efforts have been made to attract

summer visitors to this large, sprawling and unattractive ski complex. Facilities and services of every description; boating on the lake – ice floe hazard in early season. Large colonies of school children inhabit the Val Claret high-rise blocks. CAF chalet-hotel/restaurant at N end of resort, 60 places; also cheap accommodation at the Haute Montagne sports chalet. No official camping. Cableway to la Tovière, good viewpoint but not really of interest to mountain walkers. At ultimate roadhead (2107m), huge carpark on R side, in front of the Grande Motte cableway; local minibus service from Lac de Tignes centre, 3km. This cableway rises through an intermediate stage at 3032m (change cars) to a shoulder on the NE ridge of the mountain at 3440m. Reduced ticket price for pedestrians (= climbers). Only skiers are permitted to use the broad swathe ploughed and prepared by ski tractors in the gl. down to the intermediate station; this is precisely in the line of the old normalroute for climbers coming from the Col de la Leisse. Near the intermediate station, gl. slopes to the N, towards the Pramecou dome and col, are normally covered with tuition groups. Parties on foot may cross the gl. here without being challenged. Tips about how to dodge the hassle in this summer skiing area are given under the Grande Motte.

Val d'Isère   1820m

28   See R.9. On the main road, with a new dual carriage 'high street' divided by the river rushing in a deep concrete culvert crossed by bridges. An impersonal, pseudo-American downtown atmosphere pervades this celebrated resort. It was always a good mountain walking and climbing centre, long before the developers raised its buildings profile and status to undreamt of economic heights. The modesty of the larger wooden, brick and concrete edifices is due entirely to not having to create a new resort, like others in the Tarentaise. A village at a respectable altitude with good amenities already existed. Comprehensive services; prices in shops, supermarkets and restaurants reveal to the thrifty a wide variation for all kinds of purchases. Tourist office, guides' bureau, swimming pool, tennis courts, etc. Official campsite, mod. cons. etc. one km E outside resort on main road; parallel access road on S side at either end. At this height it is cold at night in summer. Possibility of bunkhouse accommodation (not officially recognised); inquire at tourist office. Numerous small, modestly priced hotels/inns.

Cableways to the Rocher de Bellevarde, Tête du Solaise, both splendid viewpoints. The latter can be reached from a carpark at pt.2406 on the Col de l'Iseran road in 15min. walking. New cableway from le Fornet hamlet on main road 3km outside the resort, to a shoulder above and N of the Col de l'Iseran; the continuation Cascade chairlift rises to the Gd. Pisaillas gl. – non skiing travellers might be refused on this

A Mont Blanc
B Sommet de Bellecôte 3417m
C Dome de Bellecôte 3381m R.174
D Dome des Pichères 3319m
E Saddle access pt. 3266 R.174
F Cul du Nant gl. R.175
G L'Aliet 3109m R.176
H Plan Séry R.50
K Aig. du St. Esprit 3419m R.178
L Upper shoulder c.3575m R.180

M   Mont Pourri 3779m   R.180,181,182,183
N   Brèche Puiseux 3469m   R.182,183
P   Dôme de la Sache 3601m   R.183
R   Dôme des Platières 3473m
V   Col de la Sachette 2713m   R.112
W   Col du Palet hut 2590m   R.46,47,48
X   Col du Palet 2652m   R.46,47
Y   Col de la Croix des Frêtes 2647m   R.48
Z   Grand Plan   R.48

stage; wave a threatening ice axe. Other chairlifts operate in summer according to snow conditions determined for skiers. Private minibus and taxi services to le Manchet roadhead, and to Pont St. Charles carpark on the Col de l'Iseran road. Inter-resort service, Val d'Isère – Lac de Tignes operates Aug.-Sept. Note: a summer cableway lift from La Daille hamlet on main road below resort to the Tovière valley at spot height 2289 provides a useful initial start for those backpacking the classic 3 cols tour from Val d'Isère to Pralognan.

Col de l'Iseran   2764m

29   See Peripheral system. Hotel and restaurant, dormitory available, souvenir stalls. Large carpark alongside skiers access road NE to the Pisaillas slopes under the Pers-Montet ridge. See Pers-Montets peaks for several problems resulting from summer skiing here.

Bonneval   1783m

30   See Peripheral system and R.10. On a parallel slip road at S foot of the Col de l'Iseran. Classified architectural site. Charming unspoiled hamlet, largely rebuilt since the ravages of World War 2, with some very old quaint houses preserved. 2 small hotels/restaurants, provision shop. Nearby, at the first bend (1808m) in the Col de l'Iseran road, junction with the Ecot lane, information centre, Pré-Cattin inn, and adjoining newly constructed (1986) CAF chalet-refuge, 14 places,etc. and cooking facilities; key at inn; recommended. No camping. Over the Arc bridge and 500m along the Ecot lane, waymarked path SE to the Criou bunkhouse (2020m) above the forest; pleasant vistas. The Ecot lane is supposed to be closed to private cars just before the Vallonnet bridge (1835m), but as recently as 1987 a guidebook survey team was able to go right up to the St. Clair bridge (2027m), under the zigzags to Ecot hamlet – another architectural site. The continuation road is closed by a locked barrier. Ecot is an ancient alpine mountain farming community which once had the reputation of being the highest inhabited all-year-round place in France. Much photographed by detouring car parties going over the Col de l'Iseran.

Bessans   1705m

31   See Peripheral system and R.11. Appealing village off main road with simple hotel/restaurant and provisioning services. No bunkhouse but one can be found at le Villaron hamlet, 2km up the road. Camp sites beside the Arc river 1.5km below village, on grassy bush-covered flats; no site amenities. A similar site can be found in the Avérole valley, entrance nearly opposite the Villaron hamlet. The road in this magnificent valley is open to cars to just beyond the campsite (R side), where an island/turning circle appears (1802m). Above this it

is closed to private cars, but motorable (taxi from Bessans often used) to Avérole hamlet (1990m). Opening just beyond the lower side of Bessans, the long, splendid Ribon valley road (unmade) is closed to everyone. (When first opened, eventually for jeeps, it was a hazardous and hardly worthwhile 2 km before you had to walk).

Lanslevillard   1458m

Lanslebourg - Mont Cenis   1387m

32   See Peripheral system. Both on the main road, 2 km apart, and directly below the zigzag ramps to the Mont Cenis pass, this area has been christened Station de Val Cenis to encourage more skiing locally. Cableways, chairlifts, skitows, of little interest as a base in summer; buses go up to the pass regularly. Both villages have reasonable services, bunkhouses and good campsites; tourist office/information centre.

Termignon   1302m

33   See Peripheral system and R.12. The most attractive village base in the Arc valley. Premier S entrance to park. Hotels/inns, shops, etc. Very popular bunkhouse, but other cheap accommodation available; caters especially for walkers/climbers. Campsite on W side of tributary river, road access N, 10 min. on foot. Small road into park, private minibus service (or taxi); this starts from sharp bend above the village at pt. 1336 and winds up for 12 km to immaculate parking place called Bellecombe (2307m). Beyond this point the road continues to the Plan du Lac (qv), and must only be used by authorised vehicles. Taxi drivers are discouraged from taking fares beyond the carpark but this advice often goes unheeded. It is even possible to pursue this road as far as Entre-deux-Eaux.

Also camping at Sollières, 3 km down the valley from village; and on the D 83 corniche road to Aussois, hotel and bunkhouse at Sardières.

Aussois   1483m

34   See R.13. Village above the Arc between Modane and Termignon, becoming quite popular, linked by separate parallel corniche road; provisioning, several hotels/inns, good campsite. Seen along terraces between village level and valley below is a string of enormous forts and military installations perched on promontories, dating back to the 19th century Franco-Sardinian confrontations. The Marie-Christine fort, one km from the campsite, is now a gourmet restaurant. Chairlift N to 2250m at the Djoin shoulder, junction with GR5 trail, generally only operates in winter. Alternative and much used EDF road to parking under Plan d'Amont barrage wall (2050m), 6 km, taxi hire. Note: in

the main valley below, at Bramans hamlet (1250m), good bunkhouse with 50 places and meals provided. Camping along lane between Bramans and Le Vernay.

Modane-Ville   1092m   Modane-Centre   1066m

Modane-Gare   1058m

35   Fairly large industrial complex spread along main road for 3 km. Comprehensive services. As you enter along the N 6 from upper E end, pleasant small hotels/inns on service road to L. An arrival destination rather than a resort centre.

Porte de l'Orgère   1935m

36   See R.14. So far the local authority has resisted building a cableway directly above Modane to this roadhead (straight distance, 3km). Popular approach from the Arc valley to the most southerly park entrance; the access road (in our opinion deliberately ill-marked) forks off 4 km below Modane-Centre, to reach St. André; it then winds back E and N through the upper forest zone to spacious parking area just above the PNV hut (14km from Modane); minibus or taxi. No camping, hut and restaurant services, qv. At the picnic bend (1770m) across the narrow opening to the Chavière valley, cars must not attempt the rough lane (GR 55) near this pt. up latter valley (Polset chalets). Beyond the carpark, one km of road further N ends at tunnel construction workings, not officially permitted to visitors with cars.

Huts and other mountain bases

Unless otherwise stated huts, etc. have a warden, staff and restaurant service. All wardened huts are furnished with a self-cooking area; in PNV huts these come with calor gas cookers, kitchen facilities, etc.; in CAF ones you must take your own stove. Unwardened PNV huts – all doors open – have cookers in situ, etc. for self catering. Payment at unwardened huts is made according to tariff charges displayed by completing an envelope-form placed with the appropriate sum in a box on the wall. Accommodation rates are considerably reduced for members of European national alpine clubs (BMC in the UK) and others with reciprocal rights. Non members can enjoy this saving by joining the Amis du Parc National de la Vanoise (only valid for Vanoise area), worthwhile if you spend more than 4 nights in huts; simple enrolment and payment procedure at the larger PNV (not CAF) huts, eg. Rosuel and Orgère. Some fresh and tinned food is sold at the park huts; meals and other services bought at all huts are the same price for everyone, with no reductions; negotiation of pension rates is possible. There is a park regulation, not strictly enforced, that no person or party should stay at one PNV hut more than 3 consecutive nights. Hut accommodation varies from large communal mattress benches to small rooms with individual bunk beds, comfortable everywhere. Generally, privacy in sleeping quarters improves with the size of the hut; inside toilets and wash/bathrooms except in the oldest and smallest buildings; electric light or calor gas lighting. At private huts (non PNV, CAF) self catering is normally not permitted; valley bunkhouses mostly allow self cooking; otherwise amenities are identical.

Between 1973 and 1985 most PNV huts had their accommodation capacity, kitchen, restaurant and other amenities/services doubled, and further aggrandisement can be expected together with opening additional sites.

Mont Jovet   2348m

37   3533W. CAF. This old site on SW side of the summit (2558m) of same name is now attained by a jeep road from Moûtiers. The small hut has been open and closed, off and on, for many years; it was open in 1988 with places for 32 and simple restaurant service provided. It is an exceptional tourist viewpoint for the Tarentaise and more distant ranges. See also R.109.

Rosuel hut

Les Bauches   1770m

38   3533E. Small private hut in a side valley above Nancroix; jeep road access; no special interest.

Chalet Bellecôte (Friolin)   2286m

39   3533E. Skitow operator's hut on N side of Col de la Chiaupe, adjoining the Plagne-Mio-Bellecôte cableway. No interest to summer visitors.

Rosuel   1556m

40   3533E. PNV. See R.23. Something of an architectural wonder, an attractive building at the Ponturin roadhead, main N entrance to park; 64 places, very well equipped, shop, etc.

Mont Pourri   2370m

41   3533E. CAF/PNV, new in 1975, replacing old Regaud hut (see below). Warden and simple restaurant service, 56 places. Situated above the Ponturin valley and below the W side of Mt. Pourri. Access by waymarked path from Les Lanches-Beaupraz (1524m), 1.5 km before Rosuel hut on valley road (road can be avoided on N side by GR 5 trail), thence easy path N and E to a junction above the Sévolière ch. (2339m). Keep R and cross the Nant Cruet stream to reach hut on a large shelf $(2\frac{1}{2}$ h).

Mont Pourri Annexe (Regaud hut)   2460m

42   3533E. CAF. Original hut site, now an empty shell with rough sleeping, no amenities, unwardened. Preferred by climbers as it is higher and closer to Mt. Pourri. From the new hut (R.41) by a traverse path SE in 30 min.

Arc chalet   2150m

43   3532E. See R.24. Private, rough road access from roadhead car park above Arc 2000; situated close to little chapel. Dormitory and simple meals.

Turia   2395m

44   3533E. PNV, no warden, 24 places. Situated on a shoulder over-looking the Upper Isère valley between La Thuile and La Gurraz. To La Gurraz hamlet (1610m) by winding service lane from br. pt. 1330m below main road (taxi only). Park cars on lower outskirts. From hamlet, waymarked Mt. Pourri circuit trail, fairly steeply N and W by the Cousset pasture to hut $(2\frac{1}{4}$ h).

La Martin   2154m

45   3533E. PNV, no warden, 33 places. Classic Isère site for Mont
Pourri, on a terrace near small, generally empty tarn-sump high above
the valley between La Gurraz and Les Brévières (1559m). See R.26.
From Les Brévières by good path NW above the lower barrage (1¾ h).
Or from La Gurraz (R.44) by a long, winding waymarked circuit S over
rock terraces and moraine (2 h); alternatively, from the neighbouring
Savinaz hamlet roadhead by steep track SW (2 h). The easiest approach is by chairlift from Tignes, above the roadbend gallery (1813m) in
Lac de Tignes direction, Boisses-Marais lift (2182m). Here a traverse
path runs N to round a corner L, where a fork R is taken to descend
across the Sache valley to join the Mt. Pourri circuit working N again
under the Rocher Blanc to hut (1¾ h). When lift is not working, a path
from the gallery bend ascends W into the Sache valley (30 min. longer).

Col du Palet   2590m

46   3533E. PNV, 48 places, separate dormitory and main building.
Situated 10 min. below W side of Col du Palet (2652m) amid pleasant
pasture surroundings adjoining GR 5 trail between the Rosuel roadhead
(R.23, 40) and Lac de Tignes (R.27). Though well marked and sign-
posted, beware of junctions for important branch paths in poor visibi-
lity; follow Col du Palet and GR 5 signs. From the Rosuel (R.40), a
clear track rising along R side of valley leads to junction L for Plan de
la Plagne. Keep straightahead at the Plagne ch. to mount above the
lake and attain in turn the Plan de la Grassaz and de Janin before
reaching the Grattaleu lake outfall (2512m); above this a short path
L behind a knoll (2565m) leads from GR 5 to the hut (4¼ h).

47   From Lac de Tignes (R.27) the path starts from road alongside the
lake and works across pastures SW and W, churned up with skitows,
avalanche barriers and service tracks, past the Lognan ch. and up a
rock slope to reach the col and a short descent to hut (2½ h).

48   From the Laisonnay hut (R.51 and Champagny roadhead, R.20),
follow main path on L(N) side of valley to the Glière chapel. When
above the meadow and zigzags N, keep R via the Gd. Plan to reach
first the Col de la Croix des Frêtes (2647m), adjoining the Palet col,
just above the hut (3¼ h).

Plaisance   2165m

49   3533E. PNV, 48 places, no warden. Situated in the Py valley
below S side of the Bellecôte massif. From small bridge just before the
Laisonnay hut (R.51), signpost, waymarked path climbs steeply N into
hanging valley (waterfall L) to reach a streambed plain where the hut
is found (2 h).

32

50   From the Rosuel (R.40), as for R.46 to junction 2068 before the
Plan de la Plagne. Keep R below steep slope on this W side of plain
to pass along W bank of lake, after which the inflow stream is forded
L (plank bridge) to continue by a steeper ascent SW in the Val de Genêt
to the Col du Plan Séry (2609m) (3¾h). Now descend the path W to
the marshy Plan Séry, then turn a corner S to cross a terrace atop steep
slopes overlooking the Py valley. A zigzag descent N round cliffs
leads to the valley plain and hut (1h, 4¾h in all; same time in reverse).

Laisonnay   1570m

51   3533E. Laisonnay d'en Haut. Private, 30 places (nearby PNV
building is not a hut). See R.20. Road terminus and large carpark beside bridge at Laisonnay d'en Bas (1559m), then along lane for 400m to
hut after a small bridge. Pleasant site.

Bois   1475m

52   3533E. PNV, 60 places. Comprehensive services at this roadside
hut in valley at Champagny-le-Haut. See R.20. Camping 500m before
hut on other side of road. People noted for dressing in local costume.

Plan des Gouilles   2360m

53   3533E. CAF, new hut directly above Champagny-le-Haut and
below N side of the Grand Bec. Popular venue for climbers, 48 places.
From Champagny valley/Bois hut (R.20,52), cross the Traye br.(1470m)
and follow steep waymarked path in forest to a series of endless short
zags between a rib L and streambed R, eventually crossing R to a stonefield, only to return L again with more of the same and unrelenting till
hut is reached at foot of the Becca Motta ridge (3h).

54   From the Plan Fournier road (1723m) (R.60), by the Méribel high
level route (no connection with the skiing site), N and E, across the
very steep vegetated Tour du Merle shoulder (1973m), down to pt.1830,
up to the Méribel ch. and a traverse/descent across the rocky base of
the Gde. Marianne ridge to join R.53 on the upper stonefield; small
track all the way (2¼h).

Saut   2126m

55   3534W. Not to be confused with Sassière, Val d'Isère ch. of same
name. Private, renovated stone and wooden building in the Fruit/
Allues valley, under S side of great rock peak of that name; a sporting
approach to the Péclet-Polset massif; a rediscovered, splendid 'lost'
valley. Normally no warden, 30 places, fully equipped, inquire at
Méribel centre or Mottaret to ensure that door is open. From the Méribel-Mottaret roadhead (1681m, R.18) continue S through a tunnel and

along a small road in the valley, past the Tueda lake (inn, restaurant, carpark, 1730m), where the trail twists up E to the Fruit ch., then into the middle valley S in a long flat, damp bed to a narrower part and a riser close to the stream with the hut just beyond a plank bridge ($2\frac{1}{4}$ h).

Lacs Merlet 2417m

56 3533W, 3534W. PNV, 14 places, unwardened. In a large, dissected cwm (Vals/Avals) between the Fruit and Portetta groups, S of Courchevel and W of Pralognan, now approached by the former's ski cable slopes. Nevertheless one of the most pleasantly remote spots in the park. The Pralognan approach lies over the Col des Saulces (2456m) or the Col du Mône (2533m), either side of the Petit Mt. Blanc viewpoint, descending to the main Vals stream, from where an undulating path W leads to hut near lakes in a hollow (5 h).

From Courchevel (R.19) by cableway to the Bel-Air (2050m) then by waymarked path S (E of a jeep road) alongside skitows to the low relief Col de la Platta (2408m). Continue more or less horizontally S round a shoulder of the Roc Merlet to descend gently to hut (2 h from cableway).

Roc Merlet (2734m). Fine viewpoint NW of hut, easily climbed by its obvious short ridges in 1 h.

Col de la Vanoise (Félix Faure) 2516m

57 3533E. CAF. The largest and busiest hut in the park, sleeps 180. Its central position astride the great depression between the Vanoise icefield and the Gde. Casse attracts touring parties, climbers and many day visitors from Pralognan. 2 prefabricated buildings adjoin the original. From Pralognan, at top of main thoroughfare turn E along road to les Bieux (1464m) to reach waymarked trail into Glière valley going up to Les Fontanettes (1644m) (45 min.). This hamlet can be reached by a road making wider sweeps, cars/taxis permitted. Follow GR 55 signs, etc. to L (ignore road R), mounting wooded slopes to the Glière br. (2005m). Continue in the open valley past the Glière ch. on a cobbled and walled-in path, soon ascending gradually to cross the Chanton br. (2210m) where zigzags on a grassy rib lead to a causeway across the Lac des Vaches under the impressive N face of the Aig. de la Vanoise (2 h). Afterwards the path swings up moraines then turns into the Vanoise trough above Lac Long. The hut is concealed almost to the last moment behind a knoll on the R (45 min., $3\frac{1}{2}$ h from Pralognan).

A popular time-saver is to use the Mt. Bochor cableway (2033m), from where a good path traverses E to join GR 55 a short distance before the Glière br. (45 min., $2\frac{1}{2}$ h to hut).

Routes to/from the Arpont, Plan du Lac, Entre-deux-Eaux and Leisse

Pierre Brune
Rocher du Col

Broes
Gaillarde

Vallonnet Gd. Roc Noir
(R.189)

2538

R 64

Lac Rond

COL DE LA VANOISE

huts are described individually under entries to these huts.

58 Descent by Arcelin valley. A parallel and popular variation for returning to Pralognan, under the S side of the Aig. de la Vanoise, and under the sheer walls of the Arcelin and Marchet peaks. Behind the Vanoise hut take a little track W and descend slightly to the Assiettes lake, going round its marshy S side (cairns only) and over small saddle to go down the Arcelin valley steeply to its upper ch. (2219m). Continue near the stream over stony ground, then with regular steepness to a junction (1881m) with the Gd. Marchet track. A moderate descent from here enters the Creuset wood and reaches the roadhead parking above Les Fontanettes at the Pont de l'Eau (1676m) ($1\frac{1}{2}$ h); then by GR 55 to Pralognan in another 30 min.

Grand Bec 2405m

59 3533E. CAF. Agreeable hut, 45 places, warden and simple meals service, mostly patronized by climbers; located on the Col de la Vuzelle, a saddle on the inner E side of the Pte. de la Vuzelle, and at the W foot of the Grand Bec. A notoriously bad path in the past, now much improved; snow cover in places to late season. From Pralognan take the cableway to Mt. Bochor (2023m). Take the path going round the L(N) side of hummock behind cableway, up a ski slope ENE to a clearly marked junction at pt. 2332 under the Creux Noir cirque. Turn L(N) to ascend round steep rocks L (cables) and across rough slopes to a rising traverse L (cables) leading to another junction on the Col de Leschaux (2564m). With a small track, a descending traverse N in a scree shoot and over rocky ground soon rises to contour the Vuzelle cwm horizontally before descending again to the Vuzelle col and hut (3 h from cableway).

60 Shortest way from Pralognan, for cars/taxis. Drive down the valley towards Planay. A short distance before this hamlet, at pt. 1189 at 5.5 km, a service road R(E) climbs in many zigzags to the Plan Fournier ch. (1723m); small parking lot here, and smaller still at roadhead beside the Bois Blanc. Go up above roadhead to join a path in a few min., running R. This mounts pleasantly SE through the forest; on emerging, cross 2 streams to reach the crest of a steep rib, climbed in zigzags to a third stream (2067m), where the track goes straight up stony grass slopes to the col and hut ($2\frac{1}{4}$ h from roadhead).

61 F+. Climbers only. From the Vanoise hut descend by R. 57 to just above the Lac des Vaches. A side path goes off R above N side of lake, traverses to the Gardes ch. (2431m) and continues over rough ground and up an icy gully (cables) to the Col Rosset (2545m). On the other side descend a steep rock jumble and a narrow stonefield into the Creux Noir cirque to reach pt. 2332 where R. 59 is joined ($1\frac{1}{2}$ h, $3\frac{1}{2}$ h hut to hut).

Plan du Lac 2365m

62 3634W. PNV, 60 places, an elaborate hut at N end of the huge terrace/pasture zone where the Termignon farmers graze animals. Road to Bellecombe parking area (R.33) continues (motorists banned) with a zigzag into a long trench, along W side of lake to hut. The GR 5 path climbs directly N and further R round a shoulder, keeping R of the road, along E shore of lake to hut (35 min.).

Entre-deux-Eaux 2130m

63 3533E, 3634W. Private, 60 places. Famous, classic Tarentaise site, at the junction of 3 valleys, much frequented. Beyond the Plan du Lac (R.62) a service road descends at length into the Rocheure valley and returns to the Renaudière br. From the Plan du Lac hut follow road, or GR5 parallel and a little E of it, to a chapel beside the road (2284m), signpost, etc. Bear L(N) along GR 5 and descend steeply round a rock barrier below to the Renaudière br. at the bottom, pt. 2053. GR 5 now goes L(W) to cross a lower bridge. However, cross this br., followed by a short ascent to chalet-hotel on R (1 h).

64 Connection to Vanoise hut (R.57). From Entre-deux-Eaux follow trail N which slants to riverbed at the Croé-Vie br. (2099m). Cross br. and mount W up a big step by a good path (GR 55), winding through rock barriers and passing an empty building called the 'blockhouse' to enter the lower end of the Vanoise trough. Go up the long bed over marshy ground and finally alongside Lac Rond to reach hut in sight from afar ($2\frac{1}{4}$ h, $1\frac{1}{2}$ h in reverse direction).

Leisse 2487m

65 3533E, 3633E. PNV, 48 places, no warden. 2 buildings, piped in water to outside trough. The Leisse valley and its river are the most notorious in the Tarentaise among walkers and climbers, and this hut ranks among the most important respites provided in the park area. It is situated at an ideal height along the interminable, dreary stony wastes. Not far below the hut site, do not rely on old snow bridges for crossing the river (several fatal accidents). From Entre-deux-Eaux go N past the Croé-Vie br. into the lower valley on GR 55 where the streambed is followed on its R side by a jeep track/path for 4 km to the Plan de la Gasta (2376m). At the back of this plain keep a sharp lookout for a good place to cross the river L, and cross as soon as possible. The map place is close to pt. 2415, where a small rib of grass and rock divides the valley. Before end July it is often necessary to wade the river in a strong current. On L side of rib the path ascends quite steeply to the hut which is situated off the path to L ($2\frac{3}{4}$ h. In descent, $1\frac{1}{2}$ h).

66   From Lac de Tignes (R.27) the service road above the Val Claret apartments enters a tunnel section near S end; just before this, the waymarked GR 55 trail starts on L, passing under the Tufs/Tovière lift and skitows and going up to the Leisse ch. (2210m). It continues SE over grassy slopes at a steady gradient to a junction near the Col de Fresse to your L. Now straight ahead through rocky hummocks and snow patches to the Col de la Leisse (2758m); traditional cairn and pole, splendid view of Mt. Blanc to N (2¾h). Cross the col along an almost level bed where the path is occasionally lost among stones and snowbeds, plenty of cairns, to enter the Leisse valley. The path passes to the L (E) of the Lac des Nettes (sometimes frozen), whose outfall is crossed (2677m) so that the R side of the stream is followed over terraced slopes to the Plan des Nettes, where the lake has been dammed. A steep descent round the Roche Blanche leads to hut on R side of the path (1¼h, 4h from Val Claret).

Note: Using the Gde. Motte cableway to its intermediate station at 3032m, the Col de la Leisse can be reached by a simple snow descent NE then E, to finish over large banks of easy slabs a short distance S of col (30 min., to hut 1¾h). Do not attempt a descent due E, or in the line of the Leisse winter ski chairlift. An administrative boundary line on the map indicates the correct descent line.

67   From Val d'Isère. This classic hike to the Leisse valley crosses what has become the Grand Pré/Bellevarde skiing grounds where the original path has been churned up by tractor roads, skilifts and winter paraphernalia. We give first our original route description, ignoring cableway options. At the lower outskirts of Val d'Isère cross the last br. on L (Pont du Crêt, 1805m) and follow a service lane R into the broad trail of GR 5 rising NW along the lower edge of the Etroits woods. This leads under the Daille cableway and round to a stream and pastures near the Tovière ch. The trail divides (2024m) and GR5 goes R to Lac de Tignes; keep L, recrossing stream L and following it to a brow leading up to the Daille sta.(2289m) (2¼h). Here another branch of the cableway ascends to a shoulder adjoining the Bellevarde lift system. The path (tractor road) continues S over grassy slopes beside skitows to a fork on the Grand Pré at c.2460m. Bear R (SW) and cross the Tovière stream depression to ascend in the line of a skitow rising to a pt. just L of the grassy Col de Fresse (2576m) (1¼h); in fact the original path passed just above 2 tarns at pt.2479. From this col a track contours SW to join the GR 55 trail near a rain gauge and before the rocky hummocks on R.66 (1h from Fresse to Leisse cols; Val d' Isère to hut, 5¾h).

Mechanically aided options are: Daille cableway to sta.2289m saves 2¼h. Bellevarde cableway (2765m), then by descending paths and tow tracks W across the Gd. Pré, and up to the Fresse col in 1¼h; saves 2¼h.

38

Other routes: From the Vanoise hut (R.57) by the Croé-Vie br., R.64, 65 (3¼ h), or with diversion to Entre-deux-Eaux, plus 30 min. From the Arpont hut (qv).

Femma   2352m

68   3533E, 3633E, 3634W.   PNV, 48 places, separate dormitory. This hut at the head of the Rocheure valley provides an overnight stage for an alternative cross-country route between Val d'Isère and the Vanoise hut/col (versus R.67,65,64). Excellent base for alpine training on secondary snowy peaks uncluttered by the trappings of skiers. From the Plan du Lac (R.62) follow service road NE, down to a T junction at pt. 2174. Continue along road E above the Rocheure valley stream; after crossing the br. at pt.2224, a jeep track follows N side of stream to hut under the Femma crags (9 km, 2¾ h).

From Entre-deux-Eaux descend the main track S (GR 5) to the Renaud-ière br. (2053m) and follow service road E into valley as for the Plan du Lac approach (2½ h).

69   From Val d'Isère. Now part of a popular high level tour across the Col de la Rocheure (2911m); often snow cover on this pass until August. A small road runs S from Val d'Isère to the Manchet hamlet (1957m) in 4 km, rough sleeping possible here, proper bunkhouse due to be opened; get a lift, or taxi hire. As the Charvet path lies on the other (W) side of the river above this pt., either cross below the hamlet by a br. at 1927m to reach an EDF service lane on W side; or join this lane at the lower Rosière br.(1915m); a taxi might take you up the lane to the EDF gallery inspection opening at c.2030m, 1.5 km beyond br. 1915m. Continue up the large track to a fork at 2124m and traverse L to cross the Charvet stream just above its confluence with the Pisset. The path ascends S, on the R (W) side of the Pisset stream, passing the Riondet ch. ruins on a platform, gathering steepness and threading up to reach the Pissets plateau and a pool. A barrier ahead is turned R (W), after which the track becomes rather poor. It winds up SE above the Pisset stream further L, then bears away to ascend directly over scree and snowbeds to reach the broad saddle of the col; extensive pan-orama, including Mt. Blanc (4½ h from le Manchet, 2¾ h in descent).

On the other side slant across W shore of the summit tarn and descend schist slopes SW to zigzags approaching the Rocheure bed below; the good path now descends more gradually above the bed to reach the hut in another 2 km (1¼ h. In ascent to col, 2 h. From le Manchet, 5¾ h; in reverse, 4¾ h).

Femma hut

Fond des Fours   2537m

70   3633E.   PNV, 48 places.   Often visited in summer for climbing the Pélaou Blanc, Méan Martin, etc., being more convenient than the old classic routes from the Pont de la Neige on the Bonneval side of the Col de l'Iseran road.   Note that the traverse of the Jave gl. and the Col des Fours (2976m) from latter br.(2528m) to the hut is a frequented exit route for guided training parties returning to Val d'Isère or Bonneval (about 4¼h in either direction, F/F+).   There is a similar unmarked route over snowfields near the Col du Pisset (2958m) to cross the divide between the Femma and Fond des Fours huts (about 5h).

From Val d'Isère to le Manchet (1957m), as noted in R.69.   The old path starts exactly in this hamlet, mounting between chalets above the road to enter the Fours valley which is followed along its L side via the Plan de l'Arselle to the Fours ch.   However, the new waymarked path crosses a br. on the road 200m beyond the chalets, then takes a short cut L to avoid 3 road bends, and follows road on R side of valley to a continuation path, past EDF workings, to join the old track just above (2303m) the Fours ch.   Now steep short zigzags S in a little gully then across a depression and up a short step leading directly to hut at the edge of a small plain (1¾h from le Manchet).

Péclet-Polset   2474m

71   3533E, 3534W.   CAF.   One of the most visited sites in the park, often overcrowded.   Beds for 80, but double this number staying overnight is not uncommon in July/Aug.   About 1/5th of visitors go on the mountain.   An old building; the kitchen, dining room and sleeping quarters are awkwardly arranged on 3 separate floors; self catering room detached from rest of building.   Going up the valley the hut cannot be seen until the last moment.   We refrain from commenting about the political penny-pinching attitudes prevailing over this site.   Pralognan to Pont de la Pêche roadhead carpark in the pastoral Chavière valley (R.16), GR 55 trail.   This valley epitomises the park concept, but owing to the number of people wandering in it you will neither see nor hear the marmottes, chamois, etc. so familiar in the other great valleys of the Tarentaise.

A little beyond the parking, cross the Pêche br. R and follow clear path on R side of valley at a generally moderate angle, with several conspicuous forks to other destinations, to a large inlet at pt.2255m where the track twists up a depression to mount a humpy, grassy spine L.   At the top of this take a prominent R fork (E), where GR 55 works ahead (S).   Ascend a steep paved path to hut on a broad grassy brow (8km, 3h from carpark).   Note: for returning to GR 55 for crossing the Col de Chavière, there is a handy traverse path S and SE to pt. 2498; it starts slightly above the level of the hut.

Génépy   2284m

72 3534W PNV, 24 places, no warden. Damaged by avalanche in
1986; check status before going. Situated above the Chavière valley,
in a cwm under the Génépy gl. A stage on the balcony trail round the
W side of the Vanoise icefield. The connection from the Fond d'Aussois hut across the Col d'Aussois is described separately. This hut allows
the Dt. Parrachée and associated summits to be climbed directly from
Pralognan. At the top of the Chavière valley carpark (R.16,71) a path
detaches L and ascends open forest to the Montaimont ch. (1900m).
Now either continue by a path S, rising steeply to the Génépy stream
gorge which is followed up its L side for some distance to meet the alternative coming from the L; or take a more gradual and longer path in
zigzags N then S, ascending and traversing into the first. Somewhat
higher the unified path bears R across the stream; a fork R from the
main track leads over another stream to the hut on R, below rockbands
(1¾-2 h from carpark). Note: hut not functioning in 1988.

Vallette   2584m

73 3534W, 3634W. PNV, 24 places, no warden. A stage on the W
side balcony trail of the Vanoise icefield, N of the Génépy (R.72),
where the magnificently rugged section N commences, called Sentier
des Cirques. Situated adjacent to col of same name, high above the
Chavière valley between Pralognan and the roadhead (R.16). From
the road at br. 1711m (park cars across br. beside the Prioux ch.) go
along road S for 300m to a track on L, returning L across the hillside.
Follow this with increasing steepness into the Nants cwm, crossed L at
pt.2045. Now the path climbs steadily past the Nants ch. (2184m) to
bear L (N) in zags across stony slopes between ravined cliffs above
and below. Some distance below the Col de la Vallette (2554m) a R
fork ascends directly to hut above S side of col (2¾ h from the road).

74 From the Génépy hut (R.72) descend the valley path, taking after
10 min. the high level route, and not the more direct way close to the
stream. Reach a fork and ruined shed on the Plan de la Sômaz, where
a traverse path N is followed beyond the last fork L down to the valley.
Now continue rising a little and crossing several small streams to contour pleasantly round a shoulder, where the path circles round the Nants
cwm to reach the Nants ch. So follow R.73 to hut (2½ h).

Orgère   1935m

75 3534W. PNV, 80 places, notably spacious self catering facilities,
etc. See R.14, 36. On foot from Modane-Loutraz by clearly marked
GR5, 3h.

Fond d'Aussois   2324m

76   3534W, 3634W. CAF, 36 places, simple restaurant service, gas in hut for self cookers. Attractive hut site in the cwm behind the twin Amont/Aval barrages and below the Col d'Aussois. From the Arc valley to Aussois, then by car or taxi to roadhead parking (2050m) under the Amont dam (R.13,34). Follow road briefly to W end of wall to where a jeep road crosses slope above the lake to reach at the far end a junction of paths at the Sétéria br. (2206m). Just over br., either take a small track L, or continue by GR 5 for a few min. to a fork L (2244m); both ways ascend NNW to the cwm plain, passing a few old ch. before reaching the hut at the back (1¼ h).

77   From Orgère hut, by GR 5, this section being called Sentier du Barbier. A short bit along road then a descent E across a narrow valley, past a chapel and round a wooded corner to commence a long easy ascent NE before levelling off to reach the rather lower Col du Barbier (2287m) (2¾ h). The path continues traversing at length N, across the lower edge of the Mauvais Berger plateau, falling a little to join a track coming from the Col de la Masse, then going straight down to the Sétéria br. on R.76 (2 h, 5¼ h hut to hut in either direction).

Dent Parrachée   2511m

78   3634W. CAF, often no warden, door open, 30 places; take your own food. Overcrowding in the 1970s led to a decision to upgrade the Fond d'Aussois (R.76) and build another hut closer to the big mountain. As for R.76; continue E beyond the Fond d'Aussois turning, along GR 5 to the next junction, 2330m near the Fournanche ch. Bear L (N) up a short, sharp track to the lower of 2 buildings on a shoulder (2¼ h from barrage carpark).

Plan Sec   2325m

78a   3634W. Privately owned, self catering and simple restaurant service, sleeping bags needed. Opened so that GR 5 trekkers could have an overnight halt between the Arpont and Orgère huts, and to discourage walkers from using the Fond d'Aussois or Dent Parrachée huts. Access from the Djoin corner on GR 5 (winter chairlift terminus), by a higher parallel path, in 30 min.

Arpont   2309m

79   3533E, 3634W. PNV, one of the most important of the park huts, constructed in split level buildings, 90 places. GR 5 is the normal approach for parties, being halfway along the E side of the Vanoise balcony trail, while climbers frequently arrive from the Vanoise hut,

or Génépy/Vallette after traversing the Dôme de Chassefôret. As many again come up directly from Termignon. From here (R.33) by small road N (D83) along E side of river to the Chatelard br. on L (1347m), 2km, taxi, lift, or walk. Signpost, waymarked path generally WNW ascends with many zigzags past various ch. to the GR balcony near pt.2095 (2¼ h). Follow trail N across ravines and streambeds, rising steadily all the way to hut in a fine position below the Vanoise/Chassefôret gl. (1 h, 3¼ h from br.).

80   From Djoin shoulder (2250m), R.78a below Plan Sec hut, one of the longest stretches of GR5, an up and down traverse of 15km round numerous spurs and deep inlets, one or two streams to ford, never rising more than 225m, or falling more than 300m in long gradual stages, all plainly waymarked. Tricky part in shale under the Corneilles rock (cables). The lowest pt. is near the end, where R.79 joins it from Termignon (5½–6h in either direction).

81   From the Vanoise hut (R.57), reverse R.64 to a fork R a short way below the blockhouse. A rocky path (Vanoise balcony trail) runs S along a huge shelf to meet GR5 at pt.2329 coming up from the Rocheure br. below; large rock table. Continue by GR5, ascending to rock pools, crossing a big moraine, streams (planks) and low ridges, with snowbeds and, in the last descent section, some slippery, icy or snowed up rock along a steep slope cut by gullies above the Doron gorge, care needed (4½ h hut to hut, in either direction).

82   From the Plan du Lac, by GR5 all the way; to lower br. R, as in R.63, followed to another br. L in 100m, until the path climbs steeply W in zigzags to join R.81 at pt.2329 (4¾ h).

83   From Entre-Deux-Eaux, descend S to cross the Renaudière br., then as for R.82 (4½ h).

84   From the Leisse hut, reverse R.65 to the Croé-Vie br., cross it and continue up GR55 (R.64) to the balcony trail fork L(S) near a memorial stone, below the blockhouse; then as for R.81 (5½ h hut to hut, about same time in reverse direction).

Cuchet   2160m

85   3634W. PNV, 24 places, unwardened. Primarily a stage on GR5 between the Plan du Lac and Vallonbrun huts. Situated directly above Lanslebourg in the Arc valley (R.32). A specially improved service path ascends N past the village water supply, to slant R into the Pramaria woods, zigzagging to exit L and crossing a traverse path to continue as GR5 with a further upward loop to the hut (2¼ h).

Mollard hut

Vallonbrun   2272m

86 3634W. PNV, 45 places, rustic 2-storey building in stone, and a popular site for day-visitors; a stage on GR 5 and the best starting pt. for the Gd. Roc Noir when approached from the Arc valley. On the main road midway between Bessans and Lanslevillard a corridor in the valley called Col de la Madeleine is crossed by a lane NW to the Collet ch. (1752m), where GR 5 comes down from the hut and hugs a steep slope to avoid the road. Alongside a chapel the waymarked path climbs N in stiff zigzags to the Mollard ch. and a T junction somewhat higher at pt. 2193. Go L (W) in a gentle ascent to pass the upper Fresse ch. and enter a grassy trough where the hut is found (2 h).

Shorter way for car drivers. Further down the main road, at the Pré Clos ch., a small road called the Grattais tourist route ascends to a specially constructed parking area at 1800m. Across a br. before the carpark a track zigzags N to enter the SW opening to the grassy trough at the lower Fresse ch. The trough leads shortly NE to hut (1¾ h).

Cuchet - Vallonbrun huts by the GR 5 balcony trail above the valley, a simple section of 1¾-2 h in either direction.

An apparently direct way between the Femma and Vallonbrun huts over the Col du Vallonbrun (3272m) involves very steep loose schist, crumbling rock steps and fairly difficult snow/ice slopes; avoid.

Mollard   2230m

87 3633E, 3634E. PNV, 14 places, unwardened. A stage on GR 5 between Bessans and Bonneval, situated among the ruined Mollard ch. due N of the Villaron hamlet in the Arc valley (R.31). At the top of the latter hamlet, a waymarked path GR 5E circles up W then N in zags, being joined by GR 5 coming from Bessans to commence at 2000m the balcony section called Méan Martin, running due N at a moderate gradient and soon reaching the hut on the R (1½ h).

FRONTIER RIDGE HUTS

Ruitor   2032m

88 3632W. CAF, 20 places, unwardened, take your own stove; keys with Mon. Mercier at La Masure hamlet. The only base, rather low, on Fr. side of frontier for climbing the Testa del Rutor. Access from upper Isère at Ste.-Foy-Tarentaise, small road to La Masure, then EDF road, narrow and winding, to Le Crot (1499m) and the St. Pierre chapel at Les Mollettes. The hut is 10 min. walk from here, near the Sassière ch.

La Motte 2030m

89 3632W. Private, 25 places, key holder in nearby ch. Take your own equipment, etc. Stage on touring route from the upper Isère, over the Col du Mont (2636m) into Italy and the Gran Paradiso park under S side of the Rutor massif. As for R.88 to Le Crot, then by good path on L (N) side of the Mercuel valley to the Motte pasture on R side in 1¾ h from Le Crot.

Le Saut Chalet 2250m

90 3533E, 3633E. Private, keys held at the Chargeur ch. 10 min. away; small dormitory, self catering with own equipment. A classic upper Isère site, primarily a base for climbing the Gde. Sassière and situated near the entrance to the middle part of the Sassière valley. From the main highway below Val d'Isère (R.28), a narrow but good road filters off at pt.1810 between the Clittaz and Sassière tunnels. This leads to the Saut ch. on R, under a small barrage. Parking for a few cars, taxi hire easy. The road continues over a br. and shortly to roadhead parking at pt.2303; camping with no services close to road. The rough road ahead in valley is banned to private cars.

On foot from Val d'Isère, walk or take a bus down the valley to an opening between the 2 tunnel gallery sections at pt.1798, opposite the Daille gorge cliffs; 4 km, dangerous on foot in the tunnels because of speeding vehicles. On the R a path goes up steeply above the Franchet tunnel, over rocky steps N to the Franchet ch. Here another path bears R, crossing the approach road 3 times before working parallel below it to join road about one km from Le Saut; further shortcuts L of the road lead to the chalet (1 h from pt.1798, 2 h from Val d'Isère).

Prariond 2324m

91 3633E. PNV, 35 places. At the foot of the Col de la Galise, before 1970 a rarely visited site except by climbers, now one of the most popular tourist venues at Val d'Isère (R.28). Local minibus/taxi service along the Col de l'Iseran road to carpark at Pont St.Charles, 5km (2056m). Road on foot, 1¼ h. From back of carpark before the br., waymarked path along E side of the infant Isère river, rising in zigzags above the Malpasset gorge, then descending slightly to grassy bed at head of the valley which is swept by several swift-flowing gl. streams. The path hugs the N side of the plain, bearing R at a fork near ruined hut, and crosses the Niolet stream to reach new hut below a big spur dividing the valley (1½ h from carpark).

Carro   2760m

92 3633E. CAF. Classic Haute Maurienne site; the most recent
improvements now cater for 100 places. Situated near the outfall of
the Lacs Noir/Blanc among boilerplate slabs under the Carro pass.
Frequent crossings between the Prariond and Carro huts by gl. touring
parties; either across the Col du Montet (3185m), or the longer, finer,
and in combination with the Gde. Aig. Rousse, double passage of the
Pas du Bouquetin (3335m) and Col d'Oin (3164m).

At Bonneval (R.30), see notes about cars and taxis; the latter will go
to the Pont St. Clair (2027m). Beyond this a rough service road continues in the valley bed to the Druis ch., where a goods transporter
lift for stone workings mounts to the Léchans ch. (3407m). On foot:
Bonneval – St. Clair br., $1\frac{1}{4}$ h. St. Clair – Druis ch., 1 h. A path N
above the Druis ch. to the Léchans ch., then a traverse W round a
spur leads to the Montet ch. junction at pt.2441 on the regular path
to hut. Walkers should leave the service road about one km before the
Druis ch., at pt.2118, waymarked path L making a steady ascent N
past the Tuilière ch. to cross the Montet stream br. (2405m), soon
reaching the junction at 2441m. The path winds up further N to angle
round the spur at 2540m and crosses the Plan Sec stream to attain a
junction with the balcony path (see below). Now more gradually E
over rougher ground to the hut ($4\frac{3}{4}$ h from Bonneval, $3\frac{1}{2}$ h from the St.
Clair br., $2\frac{3}{4}$ h from the Druis ch.).

93 By the Hte. Maurienne balcony trail, Sentier Plateau des Lauzes.
This splendid high level tour is for walkers who can get a bus, taxi or
lift from Bonneval up the Col de l'Iseran road to the Pont de l'Ouli-
etta (2476m); or for those with transport coming from Val d'Isère over
the Col de l'Iseran. Narrow spaces for cars at br. Though much longer in distance than R.92, the ascent is altogether gradual, and apart
from one descent of 100m the others are minimal. The start on the road
is quite clear, about 125m. before the br. Follow waymarked path for
10 km, large snow patches possible to mid season, joining R.92 about
one km before hut ($4\frac{1}{2}$ h, in reverse direction, $3\frac{1}{2}$ h).

Evettes   2588m

94 3633E. CAF. Another classic Hte. Maurienne site, facing the
Evettes gl. cirque. Large single storey metal prefab, 65 places. From
Bonneval, see notes under R.30,92 for reaching the Pont St. Clair.
Just before this br. a service road makes a zigzag S. At junction with
road over br. a path (signpost) shortcuts the zigzag, crosses the service
road and continues slanting SW above it in boggy ground, returning E
to a 4-way junction of paths, signpost (2332m). From here either take
a moderate path NE, E and SW, or go up directly by a steep rocky

track to where the paths unite (2469m). Continue into the grassy trough of the Col des Evettes where the main path slants L just below the top along terraces to the hut overlooking the gl. terminal moraines (3¼ h from Bonneval, 2 h from St. Clair br.).

A high level circuit between the Carro and Evettes huts, across the Sources de l'Arc, Mulinet and Gd. Martin gls., is a fairly hard but scenic touring route for keen parties (5½ h); longer than descending from the Carro to the St. Clair br. and reascending to the Evettes hut (4¾ h).

Avérole 2205m

95 3634E. CAF. Charming, popular base for day visitors and climbers, 80 places. The gl. touring route from the Evettes hut over the Selle de l'Albaron (3474m) to the Avérole, for experienced roped parties, is one of the finest in the Maurienne region; in the reverse (N) direction, the Avérole side in ascent is a bit tedious. Until the early 1970s the road up the Avérole valley was allowed to motorists but is now closed above the traffic island at pt. 1802. However, Bessans taxi drivers will take parties to the Avérole hamlet (1990m) and even to the Plan du Pré roadhead (2080m). See Bessans, R.31. From here on foot to Avérole hamlet, 2¼ h. Avérole – Plan du Pré, 30 min. At latter spot, near an EDF br. R, various paths wind up steep grass L and a few rocks to hut on a grassy shoulder in 15–20 min.

Arcelle chalet 2150m

96 3634E. Private, situated in the long Ribon valley opposite Bessans (R.31). The best Hte. Maurienne base for climbing the Rocciamelone. Most of the ch. in this vicinity are in ruins; 2 or 3 are inhabitable; so comfortable hayloft sleeping, take your own equipment. Inquire at Bessans before setting off. A lane goes out directly to main road; go along this for 7 min. to the Ribon valley jeep road on L (1732m). Follow this above the stream gorge, becoming a good path, passing several groups of ch. and grazing pasture, for some distance to the Arcelles ones in 9 km from Bessans (2½ h).

Châtel 1975m

Arcelle Neuve chalet 2203m

97 3634W. Ex. Lanslebourg and Lanslevillard (R.32). For climbing the Pte. de Ronce. Châtel hut, CAF leased, no warden, normally shut, keys at both villages. From the 3rd bend (1662m) on the Mont Cenis highway a small road makes a long gradual ascent through the Lanslebourg forest to the building a short way before the Fenêtre du Châtel; bus to the bend, then on foot, 4 km, 1½ h. Or by taxi from villages.

Arcelle Neuve chalet (no connection with Ribon valley, R.96), private with dormitory accommodation, meals possible, self catering; inquire at villages before starting out. A better place for the mountain. Some 500m distance from top of Mont Cenis pass (bus), a service road goes off NNE (la Fémaz, 2060m) and contours E under or close to several skitows above the forest (leave cars near the Tomba lift, about 1.5km). Continue across the Arcelle Neuve stream to the chalet on L, chapel, etc. (1 h from main road). On foot all the way from Lanslebourg by forest paths, the St. Pierre chapel and via pt.1734, $2\frac{1}{2}$ h.

PROJECT HUTS

Some of these have been on the drawing board for 20 years; others are noted as huts which cannot generally be used by unaffiliated visitors.

La Loza   2322m

98   3634W. On GR5, one third way along section between the Djoin shoulder and the Arpont hut (R.80), under the big signal cross 2376m. Plans by the TCF to construct a hut here beside existing ch. seem to have evaporated with the demise of this old, famous organisation.

Le Manchet   1957m

99   3633E. Roadhead S of Val d'Isère, see R.69,70. A fully equipped bunkhouse promised here (PNV, GTA or private) is awaited.

Charvet   2624m

100   3533E, 3633E. PNV. At this site beside a pool below the Grapillon tarn on NNE side of the Pte. de la Sana already stands a small park workman's building. Originally conceived as becoming a proper hut to accommodate ski mountaineers coming from the Val d'Isère lifts, $1-1\frac{1}{2}$h away, and aiming to ascend the Sana. However, few of these skiers can be tempted away from the downhill runs to contemplate this magnificent excursion over the Barmes de l'Ours and Sana gls.; the project remains unfulfilled.

Sassière lake (Santel)   2480m

101   3633E. Proposed PNV sponsored hut at top end of lake in the Sassière valley (R.90) above Val d'Isère, and under the frontier ridge between the Gde. Sassière and Tsanteleina, remains a remote possibility. This would accelerate ascents of both mountains and greatly increase climbing activity on neighbouring peaks.

Les Allues 1130m

102 3533W. CAF chalet here, for keyholders, although keys are kept in village as well; 8km below Méribel on approach road from Moûtiers (R.18). 20 places.

Courchevel skier chalet 1800m

103 3533W. CAF, in centre of resort, open all winter and spring, not normally but possibly open in summer; resident warden, 78 places.

Col de Thorens 3114m

104 3534W. Large log cabin near the chairlift head from Val Thorens (R.17). Normally used to dispense refreshments and give shelter to skiers. Accommodation not provided at present.

□

Gîte d'étape - bunkhouse; owners are often members of the national GTA association; very good simple, cheap accommodation, with self catering or meals provided as a simple restaurant service. Usually located in valleys and plainly marked on 50M and 25M maps.

Entre le Lac 2158m

Private hut beyond Lac de la Plagne, and just after the inflow stream bridge on R.50; popular day walk venue from the Rosuel roadhead.

Glière 1995m

Privately owned. At head of the Champagny valley, among the barns called Caves de la Plagne, skirted by R.48 from the Laisonnay chalet hut roadhead ($1\frac{1}{2}$h). This site is of considerable interest to climbers, for crossing the gl. pass of the Col de la Gde. Casse, and for modern rock climbs on the N faces of the various Epéna summits and the Gde. Glière buttresses.

Walking Routes, Balcony Trails, Circuits, Simple Summits

A proportion of these walks and scrambles are officially adopted tours and as such have signposts at important junctions confirming the direction to follow. These and others co-incide with parts of GR5 & GR55 trails, and their variations, so that waymarking may consist of a combination of red, white, yellow and sometimes blue paint flashes. Waymarking is not uniformly regular and a close watch must be kept on the ground for picking the best line where paths are vague and sometimes non-existent. Other tours have been devised for the purpose of this guide and use a combination of paths for various destinations.

Apart from normal mountain walking equipment, rope, axe and crampons need not be carried unless otherwise stated. Always remember that on terrain above 2400m, especially if N-facing, snow slopes of varying extent are retained throughout the season, masking paths for short distances and covering cairns, etc. at greater heights. Slabby rock above 2600m may be ice coated during the morning. There is nearly always a little snow at a moderate angle on passes above 2700m.

Most of the routes are ungraded, and therefore offer no technical difficulties, subject to the usual precautions that mountain walkers should observe anywhere in the high Alps. The exact nature of a few graded routes is explained in their descriptions.

VAL THORENS

See R.17. Before the ski developers arrived the huge expanses of meadow and pasture in this valley offered the walker a myriad of byways empty except for livestock. Now that much of the ground has been carved up by tractor roads and prickles with pylons and poles, it no longer looks attractive, and the paths, where they remain intact, look incidental to the constantly changing jigsaw of the locality. Chairlifts and cableways are the chief tripper attractions - all with splendid outlooks - Col de Thorens, Caron-Lauzon, Pte. de la Masse, and Mt. de Péclet. The classic viewpoint was always Mt. Bréquin - though now it is seriously miffed by the Caron cableway. It is approached by the Lou/ Revers tributary of the Péclet/Thorens.

Mont Bréquin   3135m

105   3534W.   F.   The main ridge summit is the N top (3130m). Axe useful, as the upper scree slopes are often snow covered to late season. From sharp bend in Val Thorens road at pt. 1882, follow a lane for 300m to where a small path descends R between old ch. to cross the Péclet stream (1867m). The path contours W to the Lou stream and a bridge where a path can be followed on W side of the valley, past the various Lou ch. (new private hut here, no details) and the lake to the Revers ch. A more vague track goes up the L (E) side of the Revers stream, SE then SSW, crossing several tributaries, to reach at the top the broad Col de la Vallée Etroite (2732m) (3¼ h). The first bit of ridge ahead is steep, so traverse and descend to the regular scree/snow slope some distance from the ridge; ascend this ground directly E into the angle between pt. 3135 and 3130 (1¾ h, 5h in ascent, 9 km, 3¼ h in descent).

Note: This mountain can be tackled more conveniently from the St. Michel-de-Maurienne/Ch. Baume roadhead in 3h. Also from the Teppes roadhead above Modane by a scrambling route of about the same duration. Col de la Vallée Etroite is an unfortunate duplication; its more famous namesake carries GR 5 out of the district due S of Modane.

MÉRIBEL - COURCHEVEL

See R. 18, 19. The remarks about Val Thorens above apply equally to these 2 ski resorts during summer. However, there are many pleasant local walks in wooded valleys, and the longer hikes to the Saut and Lacs Merlet huts (R. 55, 56) are quite popular, especially the latter - near 2 tarns in a wild cwm below the Aig. du Fruit. From R. 56, a recommended deviation is to approach the spectacular fretwork ridge of the Dents de la Portetta, sliced to its base by the narrow chasm of Br. Portetta.

The Saulire (2738m) is the chief cableway summit and viewpoint shared by both centres with lifts from both, and another from Méribel-Mottaret. Also from Méribel, the Arpasson lift (2411m) attains the ridge overlooking Val Thorens. At Courchevel a popular walking objective is the Dent du Villard, an outstanding viewpoint despite its modest height.

Dent du Villard   2284m

106   3533W.   This fine promontory divides the Courchevel (Avals) and Pralognan valleys. From Courchevel 1650 a service road SE leads in 5 min. to a waymarked path on L (Sentier des Fenêtres), dropping round forest bluffs to the valley path near a small barrage closing the Rosière lake (1522m). On the far (E) side go along lake to a signpost on the L, where a path slants across the forested lower slopes of the mountain.

(Near the barrage there are more direct and steeper tracks to join the same path higher up). Continue to a big zag R, before reaching the Rocher du Bec de l'Aigle shelter hut, and after this return L again to a junction in the forest at pt. 1889. There is now the option of going straight ahead (N) without rising until a series of short zags SE near the edge of the scarred and eroded N face (Sentier des Pins) leads to open scrub and the summit cross; or by turning R ascend with more regular steepness and longer zags to approach the S ridge which is skirted N to reach the top (3 h, in descent, 2 h). Vehicles can go to the upper end of the Rosière lake by the service road, saving 30 min.

From the Pralognan side the most direct route starts at Planay village, waymarked path W to join a balcony trail S, followed by a short ascent to the Col de la Chal (2069m); then N along the S ridge crest (3 h).

Brèche and Dents de la Portetta

107 3533W. The best approach does not adopt R.56. Either follow R.106 to the upper end of the Rosière lake (1536m) and continue up the Avals valley bed by the successive forest paths called Sentier Botanique (numbered sites above in the forest), then the Sentier des Cascades, emerging along the Plan de la Porte (jeep track) at the Biol ch. (1870m) (1½ h). Or from Courchevel 1650 centre take a path under the Bel-Air/Ariondaz cableway, soon slanting L past a reservoir to join a service road lined with apartments and leading to Pralin Mugnier and SE into the Chemin des Avals; so enter the forest by a jeep track to contour S and reach the Avals bed at pt. 1779, Plan de la Porte (1 h, or driveable for much of the distance). Coming from the Lacs Merlet hut (R.56) the Biol ch. is reached by a 4km descent through the Avals valley (1 h).

At the Biol ch. a steep track mounts SE into a shallow cwm bed beside the rock strewn slopes of les Glacerets. A number of rough zags above go into a big couloir under the Portetta gap. Go up this over scree and large blocks at a steep angle (snow possible) to the notch. (2650m) between vertical towers (2¾ h, about 4 h from Courchevel 1650). The E side (Pralognan) gully is usually icy and contains pitches of I/I+. A circuit of the Dents de la Portetta is described in R.114.

Courchevel 1650 – Pralognan forest balcony trail

108 3533W. Starting as for R.106, this contours at an uneven height right round the N side of the Dent du Villard; on the Pralognan side it rounds several spurs to descend from the subsidiary Col du Golet (the highest pt. at 2079m) to reach the valley either directly at the Croix hamlet or at a higher level across the Rocher des Fattes to join the Chemin de la Corniche which enters Pralognan itself (15km, 5½-6½h.

In reverse direction, $6\frac{1}{2}$–$7\frac{1}{2}$ h. Virtually the same time as traversing the Dent by R.106 and the S ridge).

MOÛTIERS

Mont Jovet 2558m

109. 3533W. Orientation table, etc. Massive promontory summit girt with forests and pastures, all combed with paths, forming a huge roof wedge dividing the middle Isère and lower Pralognan valleys, so united at its foot in the town of Moûtiers. It commands a glorious panorama extending from the great Dauphiné peaks to Mont Blanc, Grand Combin and Monte Rosa. The ascent can be made from at least 3 directions and by 5 separate routes. The main W spur above Moûtiers is joined by several small roads, beyond which a single lane jeep track continues to the CAF hut (R.37), 30–40 min. below the summit; 4WD vehicles only. On the Isère side the usual ways are from Notre-Dame du Pré (1270m) or the Allemands woods road (1883m); taxi possible; then to summit in 2 h. From La Plagne (R.21, and below) by an interesting series of tracks across an intervening ridge to the Pas des Brebis (2439m); 3 h to top. The classic route starts above Bozel in the Pralognan valley, from roadhead at the Cour ch. (1529m), following endless gradual zigzags NW (some shortcuts on R worthwhile) to the open slopes and CAF hut on SW side of summit (4 h).

LA PLAGNE

3533W. Worth a visit for its cableway rides to outstanding viewpoints (R.21), yet there is little of interest to the casual or serious mountain walker in this supreme skiing domain. Mt. Jovet (R.109) is easily the best expedition on foot; the track starts across pasture from the 2nd bend in road NW to the monstrous barracks called Aime la Plagne – also served by a continuous public cableway from La Plagne centre.

PEISEY NANCROIX VALLEY

Lac de l'Etroit 2166m

110 3533E. A recommendable excursion for splendid views of the Mt. Pourri massif. Behind the campsite access road, GR 5 (R.23), between the Romano and Baudin br., the forest rises densely on the S side of the valley. The old silver mines are located here. From either br. good but steep paths penetrate the forest to meet at the tarn in a pleasant bowl. Ascend by one and go down by the other; circuit from road near hamlet of Les Lanches, 4 h.

Top L: Pte. de la Rechasse (3212m) W ridge from near summit (R.151). Top R: Summit of Pte. de la Rechasse with Pte. du Creux Noir (3155m, R.167) in background. Bottom L: Fort Victor Emmanuel below Aussois village in the Arc valley. Bottom R: Val d'Isère in 1951.

The trail to the Mt. Pourri hut (R.41) is much frequented. To complete a delightful walk along this side of the valley, continue to the old hut (R.42), then a steep descent to a gradual path S to join GR5 on the Plan de la Plagne (2092m), where the GR trail is taken down the valley to the Rosuel hut roadhead (round trip from Les Lanches/Rosuel, $5\frac{1}{2}$ h).

Bellecôte circuit

111 3533E. An easy tour along paths round the Bellecôte massif, possible in 2 days but more relaxing in 3, with a short stage between the Plaisance and Bois huts. From Les Lanches/Rosuel hut (R.23,40), by R.46,50 over the Col du Plan Séry to the Plaisance hut ($4\frac{3}{4}$ h). Excellent views of Mt. Pourri, l'Aliet and the Bellecôte gls. Descend by R.49 to the Laisonnay hut and follow the Champagny valley service lane running N of the road to near the Bois hut at Champagny le Haut (R.20,52) ($2\frac{1}{4}$ h). At the W end of the service lane cross a br. and turn R along a path returning L (W) into stones between rockbands cut by small waterfalls. Take a fork R, zigzagging near the Evetta stream, to a shoulder on the L above the barriers. Keep R (NE) to reach the Tovet ch. (2120m) where the main path slants R. It is more interesting to continue straightahead up a brow to the tiny Vélière lake (2346m), and in the same NNE direction attain the Col de Frête (Chiaupe) at 2492m, under the Bellecôte cableway; unsightly machinery, etc.(3h). Descend the broad, open Mont Benin valley NNW to zigzags down to a fork; keep R by a path on R side of stream to les Bauches (1770m). Ignore service lane to L and follow another R for 300m to where a path drops down, cutting off the zigzags, to join the streambed at pt.1577, where the forestry lane to les Esserts arrives. Take this in a long gradual descent E to the campsite zone at the Romano br., 2 km below les Lanches (2h, 5h from Champagny le Haut).

Mont Pourri circuit

112 3532E, 3533E, 3632W. The most ambitious and rewarding balcony trail in the northern park area. Also conveniently started from Arc 2000, the Lac de Tignes locality, or from the Isère valley, eg. la Gurraz,but marginally better from the Nancroix valley. Extremely varied terrain, extensive views of several mountain groups, normally completed in 3 days but possible in 2 if the big descent to and reascent from la Gurraz can be sustained to start the 2nd day. The best direction, as described, is round the N end of the Pourri chain, returning round the S end, so that the Mt. Pourri hut itself is not visited.

From les Lanches/Rosuel hut (R.23,40) by R.41 to junction above the Sèvolière ch. (2339m). Ignore continuation R to Mt. Pourri hut; follow zigzags L to cross the Crête des Lanchettes in a gap (2458m), dropping

N to a terrace above a rockband on a tractor road system adjoining the Col de la Chal (3 h). The path makes a loop to the E and N, keeping L, away from 2 lakes, and descending skitow slopes by the road NW and NE to the Arc ch. roadhead (2144m). Follow the upper road NE, past the Arc 2000 buildings to where the road peters out and a trail continues across steep slopes NE to cross a shoulder. A descent near forest on the Isère side is followed by a long traversing movement SE to a junction with a path coming up from the valley. A continuous moderate ascent S soon circles round the lowest moraines of the Turia gls., crossing a shoulder near pt.2437 to reach the PNV Turia hut on a knoll (3 h, 6 h from les Lanches).

From the Turia hut descend the well marked valley path R.44 to the junction with R.45 just above la Gurraz; so by latter path to the PNV Martin hut (1½ h down, then 2 h up). This being a short day-stage, either combine with the first or next stages for completing the circuit in 2 days, or visit la Gurraz hamlet.

The good traverse path S from the Martin hut enters the Sache valley after 3 km. Cross a br. to go up L (S) side of stream through the Tignes nature reserve and reach stony slopes at the head of the Sachette cwm. The final headslope (snow) to the Col de la Sachette (2713m) is taken by a diagonal L (3 h). On the other side go down a gentle stony cwm, often with late snow, bearing R to grassy ribs leading close to the Ch. Sache. The excellent path runs down to a ch. junction at the Plan de la Plagne where GR 5 is joined. So reverse the lower part of R.46 to the Rosuel hut roadhead (2 h, 5 h from Martin hut).

ISÈRE

3632W. Quaint hamlets on E side of the valley worth a visit for those with cars include Bon Conseil (1559m), le Monal (1874m) and Chenal (1743m). The service lanes above la Thuile on the main road are very narrow, steep and winding, so great care is needed.

LAC DE TIGNES

3533E. See R.9,27. The best walks here are day trips to cols or huts; returning the same way is usual. These include R.45, started from pt. 2083 on main road in the resort; R.47; R.66. A walk can be taken to Val d'Isère following GR 5 through the Tovière valley (2 h). The latter can be varied by following an impressive track along the S shore of the Chevril lake and under the Daille gorge cliffs. By using the Daille cableway, return with a shortcut into the Tovière valley and by GR 5 to regain Lac de Tignes.

AIG. DU DÔME
above Val d'Isère

3533E, 3633E. See R.9,28. The Bellevarde and Solaise cableways offer the most advantageous access to good viewpoints, with a choice of circuitous paths for descent. The Col de l'Iseran can be reached by road or cableway. The most popular day trip to a hut is the PNV Prariond (R.91). For walkers, the incredibly steep track alongside endless avalanche barriers from the lower end of the resort, into the Picheru cwm under the pinnacled Front–Dôme peaks and to the col of the same name, is not for the nervous; hard work with a confusing giant boulder hollow and large snow patches to finish.

Front – Dôme circuit

113 3533E, 3633E. Splendid tour, quite long for a day and recommended in settled weather to fit walkers. Ice axe useful before end July for crossing the upper slopes of the Bailletta pass. Outstanding panoramic views of the Tsanteleina – Gde. Sassière groups, the Pourri, Pers–Montets–Rousse, Méan Martin and Sana groups. This circuit justifies a special visit to Val d'Isère.

From Val d'Isère walk up the main road for 2.5km to le Fornet (parking). A short way past turning R into the hamlet, reach on the road a grassy lane between stone walls on the L. Go up cobbled lane N and soon turn R onto footpath running parallel with and above road. This goes over grassy slopes above small terraced fields to rise more steeply NE across open slopes. Follow it without incident to a notable change in direction near the Couar stream, turning up to the NNW (a shepherds' trail continues NE). Higher up the path levels out and enters a zone of rocky humps and grassy bowls. Continue along a fainter track, passing the Bailletta tarn to the E, where permanent snowbeds are found. The saddle of the stony col (2852m) lies directly above ($3\frac{1}{2}$–4h).

Ignore a faint track and cairns R (E). The main path slants gently to the L (NW), though hardly more discernible at first, and frequent snow cover, to a rib beside a steep stonefield L, and with the stark Santel lake and floating ice on the R in a hollow. The rib steepens into a series of short loose zags in rocks overlooking the artificial Sassière lake. At the bottom of this section a better path crosses a steep slope NW, then a stream, to a junction with the Picheru (Dôme) track, before dropping gently towards the Sassière barrage. Keep L along S side of the Sassière valley, where a pleasant path reaches the stream, then the Saut lake and Saut ch. under its barrage (2h). Now reverse R.90 to Val d'Isère ($1\frac{1}{2}$h, allow 8h for round trip).

Pélaou Blanc 3135m

114 3633E. Designated by PNV as Tour du P.B., something of a mis-

nomer because summer visitors, rather than traverse the Col des Fours under the S ridge of the mountain, usually attain the summit by one way and descend by another. Before August steep snow can be encountered on any approach, altogether variable, when the grading can be put at PD; in good conditions, F. The Val d'Isère tourist office organises a few guided party trips with up to a dozen persons in one group for a modest charge inclusive of transportation. The ascent and descent are made the same day. A very traditional modern excursion, outstanding panoramic viewpoint, highly recommended. Ice axe needed.

The soft option uses the Solaise cableway, followed by the Cugnai lift which normally operates in summer only to end July. Now at 2880m, ascend the steepish L side of the Ouillette NW ridge on snow and rock to this summit (3082m). Continue S, keeping to R side of crest on rotten rock down to the Col de la Calabourdane (3006m) and reascend similarly to the Pte. de l'Arselle (3110m). Again keep mostly R (W) along ridge dropping to the Col de l'Arselle (3039m) and finally climb the rock ridge above on its R side then along the blocky crest to top of the Pélaou Blanc ($2\frac{1}{4}$ h from chairlift terminus).

It is usual to descend the much steeper S ridge to the Col des Fours (2976m). There is a steep rock bit and possibly a similar pitch on snow before reaching the triple col; go to the furthest S gap, large cairn (30 min.). On the W side descend a rough rock slope with a good path soon appearing and running down steeply to the Fond des Fours hut, for lunch (1h from col, $1\frac{1}{2}$ h from summit). Thus return by R.70 to the road at le Manchet, and Val d'Isère ($1\frac{1}{4}$ h, or without transport le Manchet to Val d'Isère, add 50 min.).

If the Cugnai chairlift is not working (conditions for skiing dictate this operation) the considerable stretch between the Solaise and Cugnai top sta. is taken by paths SE and over br.2508 to join a track near skilift system above the Moutons carpark on the Col de l'Iseran road. Ascend track and near the top leave it so as to pass head of skilift and work up R (S) over a gl. slope to join ridge at back, just R of pt.3032. By this NE ridge of the Ouillette soon reach latter top ($2\frac{1}{4}$ h for this section from the Solaise, compared with 40 min. from the Cugnai terminus).

Local guides favour a route from the Col de l'Iseran (R.29), by rocky NE ridge of the Pte. des Lessières (3043m), abysmally loose in places and with several short and easy rock steps, then by the continuation to the Ouillette ($1\frac{3}{4}$ h for this section).

The classic route, and the one used to 'tour' round the Pélaou Blanc, leave the S side of the Col de l'Iseran road at the Pont de la Neige (2528m), following a cairned line SW on to the flat Jave gl. At the top a saddle to the R (W) is reached, then a steep traverse SW, often snow, leads to the Col des Fours, where the S ridge is taken to summit ($2\frac{1}{2}$h from road, $1\frac{3}{4}$h in descent, F+).

PRALOGNAN

See R.1, 16. A great diversity of excursions is possible from this centre. Hut walks and hut to hut connections are as popular as any, and for these reference should be made to the following routes: 57, 58, 59, 60, 61, 64, 71, 72, 73, 74, 106, 108. Visitors to the Vanoise (Félix-Faure) hut should note that the easiest routes to the Aig. de la Vanoise and the Pte. de la Rechasse, though technically easy, are really only for experienced tourers familiar with rock pitches and crevassed slopes.

Petit Mont Blanc   2677m

115   3533W, 3534W. Exceptionally fine viewpoint above the Pont de la Pêche carpark (R.16). Lower down to the road very steep tracks go up the cliffed flank of the Chavière valley; the furthest N of these is acceptable for descent. Start along R.71; after 15 min. and before coming to the Motte ch. a waymarked path forks R (N); follow this with a gradual ascent over grass and scree, past a junction (2116m) to zigzags rising at length to the Col du Mône (2533m) (2 h). A small twisting track goes up the sharp S ridge to the top in another 30 min. ($2\frac{3}{4}$h from carpark). The descent can be varied by going down a similar track on the N ridge to a junction with the Col des Saulces at pt. 2371. Continue down this path, very steep in places, to the road at the Planes ch., 3km below the carpark and therefore halfway down to Pralognan ($2\frac{1}{4}$h in descent).

Dents de la Portetta circuit

116   3533W, 3533E. See also R.107. A tour under these striking limestone towers. A stiff excursion but well worthwhile for strong walkers. It is not unusual to start by traversing the Petit Mt. Blanc R.115. From the Planes ch. on the road midway between Pralognan and the Pont de la Pêche carpark (R.16), waymarked path W to the Col des Saulces; follow this into woods with continuous short zags to emerge at the Saulces ch., then gentler slopes to a steep headwall rising to a junction with the Petit Mt. Blanc N ridge at pt. 2371. Now a short way from the actual col, soon slant above the path and work N up a narrowing grass slope to a stony shoulder with large cairn at the top, pt. 2835. This shoulder and the scree tips skirting it below are known as the Passage de Plassa ($3\frac{3}{4}$h). Under the W side of the Plassa ridge, descend N along a rough hanging boulder slope/ramp, under the Col and Aig. de Mey to join the boulder track under the Br. de la Portetta (R.107). After visiting the latter descend the zigzags of R.107 to

c.2300m then make a rough scramble N across the top of the Glacerets zone to reach another track coming from below and rising to the Col de la Gde.-Pierre (2403m) (1½ h). From here descend the earthy Pierre couloir NE to join the balcony trail mentioned in R.106 at a 4-ways junction. Do not go straight down to la Croix. Continue the upper traverse SE in forest, passing behind the Fattes promontory (1839m) and down to a fork; keep R and descend to the Chemin de la Corniche; follow this SSE to le Plan on the outskirts of Pralognan (1½ h, round trip about 7 h).

Marchet tour (Sentier des Cirques)

117 3533E, 3634W. Another perambulation among astonishing lime-stone cliffs, good track most of the way in steep rugged slopes with several easy rock pitches where the cols dividing a series of cirques are often snow covered to late season; ice axe advisable. A shorter version is quite comfortable for a day, but the longer circuit can be done in 2 days, using the PNV Vallette hut. Do not go in rainy weather when stonefall can occur.

Start from the Pont de l'Eau carpark (1676m) a little beyond les Font-anettes, R.57,58. Cross the br. and ascend to the bed of the Arcelin cirque, going up to a waymarked junction at pt.1881. Turn R (S) and climb a very steep track with cut steps and rails, approaching the Dard stream which is crossed by planks (2078m) to wind up spectacularly into a narrow opening between soaring ridges of the Gd. Marchet and Pet-ite Aig. de l'Arcelin, where the Cirque du Dard is entered. The track steepens in rocks to exit up a headslope W over terraced slab and grass patches at the Col du Gd. Marchet (2490m) (3¼ h). (A little to the N the Gd. Marchet E peak is quite tricky and grade III). On the W side of the col descend steep zags over stony grass slopes into the Gd. Mar-chet cirque, nearly level along the bottom to a junction near pt.2209. For returning directly to Pralognan keep R and descend W round the lower cliffs of the Petit Marchet, crossing a terrace band before drop-ping steeply through the last crag below by an equipped section called the Pas de l'Âne where a stone staircase is found in a little chimney/gully. Now either go straight down NNW in the forest to the service lane bordering the forest and campsite, or at 1700m in the forest take a R fork making a descending traverse NNE down to the Gavin br. and small road entering Pralognan (2¼ h, 5½ h for round trip).

To continue the longer tour, at the fork near pt.2209 return L and zig zag up SW to pass round a narrow terrace in the Petit Marchet cliffs (cables) to reach a slope below the Petit Marchet cirque. Now joined by a track coming from the Pas de l'Âne, ascend grass and stones S to a T junction. Traverse R (W) and slant R up a rockband extending down from the Roc du Tambour (cut steps, stanchions) to reach a grooved slope above terraced rocks, leading briefly S to cross a shoulder called Col du Tambour near pt. 2499. After a short descent and reascent to within 100m distance of the Col de la Vallette, a track L goes to the Vallette hut in another 5 min. (1¾ h, 5 h from carpark).

Descend by R.73 to the Chavière valley road near the Prioux br. 1711m in 1¾ h, about one km below the Pont de la Pêche carpark and about 1 h on foot by the road and GR 55 trail down to Pralognan (round trip in a day, allow 9 h).

ARC VALLEY

Bonneval

118   3633E. This hamlet (R.30) is more of a departure pt. than a resort centre. Principally visited for access to the Evettes, Carro and Mollard huts, R.87, 92, 93, 94. From the Evettes hut, the Evettes gl. can be explored as far as prudence allows by a well marked path S, and a return to the valley made through the Reculaz gorge. Most cairned routes above the Carro hut soon lead to snowbanks, though the Col du Carro (N) (3122m), 1¼ h, and the Col des Pariotes (SE) (3057m), 1¼ h, are worth the effort for the superb panoramas revealed.

Bessans

119   3633E, 3634E. See R.31. Hut walks include the Vallonbrun and Mollard by GR 5 (R.86,87) and the Avérole (R.95). A pleasant walk lies in following the Ribon valley (R.96) and returning the same way. In the forest above the campsites, a circuit by an upper track called the Chemin des Alpes, starting near the Ribon br., descending after 3 km to the Chantelouve ch., and returning along a lower forest path near the Arc river, called the Chemin du Petit Bonheur, offers 3 h of gentle pastoral exercise.

Lanslevillard

120   3634W. See R.32. The Vallonbrun hut (R.86) is probably the most popular excursion. On GR 5 midway between the Cuchet (R.85) and Vallonbrun huts, a waymarked track winding generally N towards the Gd. Roc Noir leads to the Pierre aux Pieds neolithic rock site (2740m) by contouring a hollow and zigzagging steeply up a weakness in a rockband to reach this large schist boulder on an open slope (2½ h from either hut). Pock marked with holes and the engraved impression of human feet, the precise origin of this megalith has not been determined. Only mount the stone in stockinged feet (preferably not at all).

3078

Rôteau d'Aussois

Col de la Masse

R. 123

R. 123

Dent Parrachée hut

Termignon

121 3634W. See R.33. The hut walks are particularly attractive –
especially combinations of R.62, 63. 79, 82, 83 (Plan du Lac, Entre
deux Eaux, Arpont). Lanserlia lakes (Col de Lanserlia, 2774m). This
frequented lunch spot is attained from the Bellecombe roadhead (R.33)
by following the GR5 trail E for one km, till after crossing the Piou
stream a faint track on L (NE) climbs fairly steep grass slopes into a
narrow stony trough leading to col; the lakes lie among hillocks on the
other side (1¾h). Possible to descend NE and N to the Rocheure valley service road and return by the Plan du Lac (R.68).

On the S side of the Arc valley a distant viewpoint is the ruined fort
(one of many) perched atop Mt. Froid (2822m). A forestry road system
attainable either from Termignon or Lanslebourg sweeps back and forth
in the dense Arc forest up to a forestry hut at the Replat des Canons
(2098m), suitable for small cars, taxi hire. From here a further stretch
of jeep road with shortcuts for pedestrians leads S to the immense Sollières pasture. This is crossed in a rising traverse S by paths at 2 levels,
to join at the Col de Sollières (2639m). A set of steep zigzags W goes
up to a prow at an old fortification, then a track on R (N) side of the
ridge leads to the Mt. Froid summit; extensive panorama (3¼h from
forestry hut/roadhead). The forestry road can be followed E to join
the Mt. Cenis road at 2000m.

Aussois

122 3634W. See R.34. Hut walks and sections of GR5 provide the
best hikes, viz. R.76, 77, 78, 80 (Fond d'Aussois, Dt. Parrachée).
Motorable forestry road NE to massive obelisk (3min. on foot) in the
forest above Sardières, called Monolithe de Sardières (1695m). This
geological wonder is about 98m high, 1¼h on foot from Aussois; picnic
place. Climbers note: grade V, A1/2, tricky abseil descent. A classic
pass hereabout to Pralognan is the Col d'Aussois (2916m), considerably
rougher than GR55 over the Col de Chavière, but now with a much improved path; frequent late snowfields, steep but otherwise technically
easy (2h from Fond d'Aussois hut); view includes Mt. Blanc and the
Chasseforêt/Péclet groups.

Râteau d'Aussois 3131m

123 3534W, 3634W. Splendid, rewarding scramble on steep, rocky
and boulder strewn ground, late snow cover common; axe advisable, F.
From the Sétéria br. (2206m), reached from the Amont carpark in
ascent, or from the Fond d'Aussois hut in descent, by R.76(30–45min.),
ascend SW by GR5 to the prominent plateau junction with the Col de
la Masse track, noted in R.77. Leave GR5 and continue due W by

increasingly steep grass then rubble slopes cut by little rock barriers, into a stony scoop. Bear L (S) and follow cairns up a broken rockslope with steep snow ribbons to the broad Col de la Masse (2903m) at the top ($2\frac{1}{2}$ h). Now a rocky slope flanking the N ridge further L is taken with snow plaques, keeping slightly L to join latter ridge above the Petit Râteau shoulder (3101m); then by the ridge itself to S end with cairn, etc. (45 min., $3\frac{1}{4}$ h from Sétéria br., 2 h in descent).

Orgère

124   3534W. See R.36,75. A nature trail circuit (Sentier Ecologique), occupying 2 h of gentle strolling along captioned slopes of flora and encapsulated natural history is the most popular outing at this hut site. A GR5 variation N leads easily from the road beside the hut to the stony Col de Chavière (2796m), having joined GR55 at pt.2504 some $1\frac{1}{4}$ h before the pass is reached ($3\frac{1}{2}$ h from hut, $2\frac{1}{4}$ h in descent). Fine view of the Écrins massif and Mt. Blanc. This pass is the highest crossed by any GR route in France, and links Pralognan and Modane as GR55, coming down to the Polset ch. and the access road to the Orgère hut about 2 km before the latter, as noted in R.36. Pass to Péclet-Polset hut (R.71), $1-1\frac{1}{4}$ h in either direction.

124a   The easiest worthwhile scrambling peak from the Orgère hut is the Râteau d'Aussois (R.123). To reach the Col de la Masse, follow road N to engineering works terminus; cross a stile on R and cross the stream at head of valley plain (1965m), leading past the nature trail (a turning S) to ascend the R side of the continuously steep front of the Masse valley NE by a good but small track in countless short zags, to enter the rocky hanging cwm between the Aig. Doran (L) and the Râteau (R). Go right up into the narrows formed between a rognon called la Masse (2951m) and the R bounding ridge; snowbeds. Bear away R (E) and ascend to ridge at pt.2923. A short rocky traverse and descent (cairns) on L (E) side joins the last bit of track/cairns of R.123 going up again briefly to the Col de la Masse (2903m) (3 h). Then as for R.123 to summit (45 min., $3\frac{3}{4}$ h from Orgère). F, axe advisable.

The most satisfying circuit from the Orgère hut is to ascend the Râteau (as above) and descend from the Masse col as for R.123 to the prominent plateau junction with GR5. From here follow GR5 as for R.77 across the Mauvais Berger plateau and the Col du Barbier to return to the Orgère (round trip, $8\frac{1}{2}$-9 h, or without climbing the Râteau, say $7\frac{1}{2}$ h).

Selected Standard Mountain and Rock Climbs

AIGUILLE DE PÉCLET 3561m

AIGUILLE DE POLSET 3531m

3534W. Equally popular ski mountaineering and summer gl. excursion.
The rotten nature of the Péclet rock has been previously understated.
Notable regional and distant panoramic views. Polset: W. Mathews
with M.A. Croz, 5 September 1861 (the resolution of doubt about this
ascent is settled by Coolidge in AJ XII, pp.269-270). Péclet: W.A.
B. Coolidge with C. Almer father & son, 12 August 1878.

125 Polset Normal Route. Climbed more often than all other routes in
the group put together; very fine gl. expedition, normally easy, though
variable crevasse complications on lower part of gl. F+, axe, crampons
needed. From the Péclet-Polset hut (R.71) a path slants NW in turf to
cross a shoulder and contours slabby rocks above Lac Blanc to continue
gently WNW to a steeper slope and loose rubble leading up to a little
plateau dotted with white rocks, flanked by a large moraine L (S), and
the Col du Souffre opening ahead. Follow marker cairns bearing L to
a boulder trough under inner side of moraine; ascend moraine flank by
a vague track to its crest and follow this till it peters out in rubble on L
side, beside the Gébroulaz gl., still some distance below end of rock
spine, pt.2943 (1¾ h).

Ascend the gl. in 2 or 3 short steep crevassed steps to a vast snow plain
above this first section. Go up it bearing a little R then L (SSE) into
the broad trough between rock spines 3267 (L) and 3302/3400 (R). At
length emerge on a plain snow brow and ascend directly S to cross a
small bergschrund under pt.3501 (the Dôme). A steep snow tongue and
rocks attain this top. Descend across a snowy hollow due W, reach the
main ridge L and climb a few rocks to the Aig.de Polset pinnacle (2¼ h,
4 h from hut). The Dôme can be avoided by contouring below it to enter
the snowy hollow (saves 15 min.).

125a From Saut hut (R.55), rather long but gradual and altogether pleasant. A fair path follows R side of the Allues valley S to a junction on
moraine below the Gébroulaz gl. Keep straight ahead (S) up moraine
beds R of a trench and cross head of trench L to follow up the E bank of

From the Aig. de Polset, looking S across the Chavière gl. to the Écrins massif in the distance.

A   Dôme de Polset 3501m   R.125
B   Aig. de Polset 3531m   R.125
C   Pt. 3400   R.125
D   Pt. 3267   R.125
E   Pt. 3515
F   Aig. de Péclet 3561m R.126,127
G   Pt. 3534   R.128

POLSET   PÉCLET

A   B C   D   E   F   G

Gébroulaz gl.

the gl. Pass a cairned fork L for the Souffre col and work up gutter S between ice and moraine to crevasses round the rock peninsula 2943m. Bear L here, over a contorted part of the gl. to join in a short distance R.125 above its initial gl. steps ($3\frac{1}{4}$ h, $5\frac{1}{4}$ h to summit).

Péclet East Flank of North Ridge. The old normal route from the Péclet–Polset hut. Not recommended, very loose and the large square snow patch under the ridge at pt.3534 is exposed to morning sun and avalanche prone.

126 Péclet Revised Normal Routes. From the Péclet–Polset hut this is best done by traversing the Polset to the Gébroulaz col, though latter can be reached directly up the larger W branch of the Gébroulaz gl. - with a number of long, wide crevasses and small séracs - turning the last rock island on the L (E) side to return steeply R across a snow shoulder to gain the col (saves 30 min.). Either way, F+.

As for R.125 to top of the Polset (4h). Descend the rock and snow ridge WSW, a bit loose and sometimes icy, to saddle in front of pt. 3511. Leave the ridge and circle down a snow slope NW and WSW to reach the Col de Gébroulaz (3434m) (30 min., 45 min. in reverse). Descend the 40° headslope W, sometimes shale exposed, for 50m to the upper basin of the Chavière gl. Track NW under the SE ridge of the Péclet for a few min. to below the S facet, R of the summit line. Climb steep loose shale, bits of track, trending R to the SE ridge, then similar loose rock on ridge to top of Péclet (45 min., $5\frac{1}{4}$ h from hut).

127 Péclet Val Thorens side. F/F+. Start from head of chairlift at the Col de Thorens (3114m) (R.17,104). A short rock spine leads on to the Chavière gl. plateau; ascend this NE with a steeper and somewhat crevassed part to the upper basin below the Gébroulaz col further R. Bear L and join R.126 at foot of S facet rocks ($1\frac{1}{2}$ h from chairlift/col to top).

128 Péclet North Ridge. Owing to cableway developments at Val Thorens, now climbed quite often. This deceptive, low relief ridge is composed of terrible rock; on account of this, PD+. Start from head of Péclet Gl. cableway (2940m), R.17. Above, a skitow system continues to a ridge shoulder at pt.3301 - climbers cannot use this. Ascend diagonally L along a broad ski piste and after 10 min. return diagonally R to skirt up the L side of a rock island supporting tow pylons, halfway up to ridge. Now go up directly in line of skitow to wooden platform on ridge (45 min.); thus far dull but easy. Now on the ridge either follow large loose blocks on or near crest, or better, stay on R side along upper edge of gl. snowfield (rotures), and join crest after 250m distance. Continue on crest, soon with a short steep step normally taken by an icy

groove or ribbon on R with loose holds. A mixed crest of shattered
blocks now leads to pt.3534, then more loose rock, gingerly along a
narrow crest with snow edges to the forepeak (1h). A deep gap cuts
off progress. Come back a few paces and descend abominable shaly
rock on R (W) side for 30m to a gap at the uppermost edge of the icy
Péclet gl. Reascend the other side on snow and rock to true summit
(15 min., 2h from cableway; in reverse, $1\frac{1}{2}$ h).

129 Péclet West Face. A snow/ice climb of 600m above Val Thorens,
up the middle of the S branch of the Péclet gl. with crevasses, bulges
and séracs according to season; reasonably sure conditions before end
July. Continuously steep, AD-/AD+. H. Mettrier with J. Antoine,
J. Favre, 28 June 1907.

POINTE DE L'ECHELLE 3422m

3534W. Imposing rock hulk resembling a tilted gable roof. Rock only
fair, some good. Climbed frequently since the Fond d'Aussois hut was
opened, also reasonable from the Péclet-Polset and Orgère. A. & P.
Puiseux, 14 July 1884 (gully in R side of SW face, not recommended).
W.A.B. Coolidge, F. Gardiner with C. Almer son, R. Almer, 30 July
1889.

130 North Ridge. Traditional normal route, PD. H. Ferrand with
C. & P. Roderon, A. Damevin, 11 August 1891. From the Fond d'A
hut (R.76) follow the good track WNW towards the Col d'Aussois, to
the rockbands where the track turns generally N. Cut off L and go up
grass, scree and rocks SW with bits of a track to snow patches under the
low relief saddle of the Br. de la Croix de la Rue (2928/9m) ($1\frac{3}{4}$ h).
Slant up L to avoid saddle and climb a short scree/snow gully to near
the ridge crest. Continue on this E side of crest along snowy ledges
and ramps parallel with crest to a shoulder on ridge itself, where the
ridge line becomes S-N. Continue slightly L of crest (loose) below a
steep step, then the ridge itself to the top ($2\frac{1}{2}$ h, $4\frac{1}{4}$ h from hut).

131 From Péclet-Polset hut (R.71) descend the approach track for 5
min. to GR 55. Follow latter for a few paces to a cairned fork L; so
contour and descend steep grassy slopes SE with a vague track in parts,
then rocks and boulders to moraine below the Masse gl. Follow main
moraine ridge SE and at the top bear L under a slabby buttress R to
enter a gully by steep snow. Climb this over big blocks and with two
pitches (II) near the top to the Br. de la Croix de la Rue ($2\frac{1}{4}$ h). Then
keep to L side of ridge and join R.130 ($2\frac{1}{2}$ h, $4\frac{3}{4}$ h to summit from hut).

132 South-South-East Ridge. F+, the easiest route. From the Orgère
hut, as for R.124a to the Col de la Masse (3h). Or from the Fond d'A.

PTE. DE L'ECHELLE

Br. de la Croix de la Rue
N' ridge
3345
R.130/1
2639
Masse gl
3125
2756
GR 55

hut by R.123 (2½h). From nearby pt.2939 follow easy rock spine N to a snow shoulder, above which a steep snowy/rock facet leads to the Gd. Roc promontory (3316m). Continue along the main ridge over large blocks to a series of little buttress/steps giving pleasant scrambling to the almost horizontal summit crest (2¼h, 5¼h from Orgère, 4¾h from Fond d'Aussois).

AIGUILLE DORAN   3041m

3534W. Popular rock climbing peak of firm smooth granite. The N-S crest is very sharp and the summit consists of 2 overhanging flakes. R. Godefroy, solo, 28 June 1891. C.F. Meade with P. Blanc, July 1920.

133 Traverse North-South. The approach to the Col du Ravin Noir (2941m) is a bit excessive, but when you get there the excellent rock compensates for the effort. III+/IV. J. Capedon, L. Comberousse, V. Cordier, E. Piaget, 11 October 1908. From the Orgère hut as for R.124 to below the Masse rognon and Col de la Masse. Cross the valley W and traverse on to the very steep slope below the obvious Col du Ravin Noir. Ascend tediously over loose scree and fine grey earth with footstep grooves, for 150m to the saddle (3½h).

Follow N ridge to a little gap, then stepped ledges on L side to a rock head overlooking a gap 15m below. Abseil or climb down (III) astride; protection peg in place. A further section L of crest and a cracked slab give access to a V gap. Climb a 5m wall (III+); or by a footledge R and a slab (III+). Continue along sharp crest, astride it or by hand traverses (III), and with a short step (III) reach a little saddle under summit step. Descend slightly on the R side by a gully/ledge system to foot of an obvious steep chimney. Climb this (12m) with an awkward chockstone (peg, IV) to exit R along a ledge line, followed by a cracked slab (II+) to top (1¾h).

Go down S ridge on R side, along a corniche of slabs (II) to a step above the Mauvais Pas gap. Either abseil 10/15m, or descend R(W) side, between 2 flakes, then 6m down a short cracked slab to return 3m L (facing out) over slab to gain crest 2m above gap (III/III+). So from here by the crest at length, turning a lower step L or R, to reach the Lower Gap (II+). It is more usual to descend the slabby R(W) side for a short way, then to cross terraces, ramps and slabs obliquely to the gap; a similar movement can be made on the L (E) side. From the Lower Gap so attained, just N of pt.2771 (1¼h) a broken rib (I+) falls W, down to scree and boulders; lower still cross the Povaret stream (2398m) to contour SW/S, slightly upwards, to join the GR 5 var. track coming from the Chavière col and leading directly to the Orgère hut (1½h, round trip 8-9h).

All pitches are variable except the chockstone chimney. To reverse N ridge, the summit step can be abseiled to little crest saddle so noted. Approach from Péclet-Polset hut, across the Chavière col by GR 55, a traverse near S corner of the Partie lake, then scree and gully ascent to Ravin Noir col ($3\frac{1}{4}$ h, but $3\frac{3}{4}$ h in reverse). There are a number of harder technical climbs on the W face of the Aig. Doran.

DENT PARRACHÉE 3697m

3634W. Huge complicated mountain, notorious for its uniformly wret-ched schist-like rock; contrari-wise, nowadays a summit much in vogue. The view is of unparalleled magnificence. Sardinian surveyor and 2 hunters, 1862. T. Blanford, P. Cuthbert, E.P. Rowsell with J.V. Favret, A. Deymoniez, J. Gizioz, 3 August 1864.

134 <u>West Ridge</u>. The normal route, loose brittle rock, always prefer-able when covered with frozen snow; delicate narrow summit ridge in a fine position, sometimes corniced, PD. The Dt. Parrachée col at c.3300m lies just E of pt.3338. From the Dt. Parrachée hut (R.78), return along the access path for a few m. to a cairn on L where a little broken track traverses grassy slopes E into the Fournanche valley. Go up the broad bed NE, bearing L (N) up increasingly rough ground with cairns into the L-hand upper cwm below the col. Scramble up quite bad, shifting scree and schist into a snow/rock couloir (stonefall) and climb this ($35°$) tediously to col ($2\frac{3}{4}$ h). Var: about 15 min. after lea-ving hut, mount due N and go round L (W) side of the rounded Gd. Châtelard promontory (2817m), near a streambed, to return bearing R by a rising traverse into the upper part of the Fournanche valley (15 min. shorter). Many parties have also gone up the parallel Eché ridge to the main W ridge W of pt.3338 - a little longer and only slightly more comfortable.

From the col follow a track in schist and rocks on crest to below a step, where a turning movement over bad rock and (hopefully) snow is made on the steep L (NW) flank. Continue below crest and slant across steep rock/snow to a rib adjoining NW couloir of the Pte. de la Four-nanche; climb this and exit up a stony gully to main ridge close to the latter Pt. (3639m). The curving ridge ahead, above the NW face, is usually snow, narrow and corniced in places on R (SE) side; at the top move R up a few rocks to summit ($1\frac{3}{4}$ h, $4\frac{1}{2}$ h from hut).

135 From the Arpont hut (R.79) go S along GR 5 for 3 km to the Mon-tafia shoulder. Now ascend the shoulder W for a similar distance and latterly on the R side slopes, approaching the Grand Pyx stream, to reach a moraine terrace under the Mahure gl. Go up R side of the gl. with a crevassed zone further L, to join the central bowl, working S

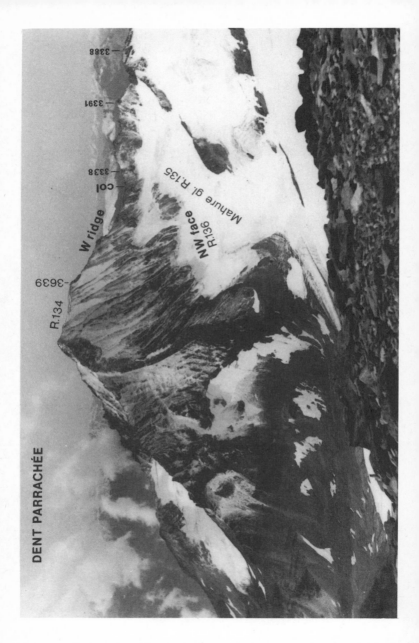

DENT PARRACHÉE

R.134
3639
W ridge
col
3338
3391
3388
Mahure gl. R.135
NW face
R.136

and SSW to a slight steepening below a rock barrier at the top; variable longitudinal crevasses throughout. Under the Col de la Dent Parrachée, a gully slope is seen R, behind a little buttress. Climb the steep, unpleasant bed to col ($4\frac{1}{2}$ h), then as for R.134 ($6\frac{1}{4}$ h from hut to summit), PD.

An alternative approach from hut follows R (N) side of the Ile stream to the Arpont gl. tongue. Cross this S to traverse round a ridge S and SW to reach the Mahure moraines.

136 North-West Face. Picturesque tapestry of ribs and gullies above the Mahure gl., approached by R.134/5 across the Dt. Parrachée col, or by R.135 from the Arpont hut (either way, $3\frac{1}{2}$ h). The Col de Labby (3328m), R.159, is an easier alternative from the Dt. Parrachée hut ($3\frac{3}{4}$ h). In the last 50 years this face has become progressively denuded of snow, leaving mostly ice ribbons in the gullies after mid season. The alternating rock ribs of undercut laminate are terribly loose; stonefall danger. The average angle everywhere is $50/55^{\circ}$, except on the R side under the Pte. de la Fournanche. The original route took a rib starting at c.3130m, a few m L of the top of a gl. inlet in the summit line and finished on the W ridge about 5 min. from the summit; 550m, D/D+. H. Mettrier with J.A. & J. Favre, 17 July 1907. A gully system R of this rib was climbed by R.G. Collomb, R. Dangerfield in 1952. Just L of the Mettrier rib a very steep gutter mounts the face to finish a few m from the summit; ice ribbons at 55°, avoidable on bad rock at IV+, generally D, 600m. J.C. Poulin, J.N. Roche, 25 December 1973. Times to accomplish these climbs vary from 5 to 9 h.

The only recommendable gully route is the broadest one at R side of the face, under the Pte. Fournanche. One must traverse from the upper gl. bowl to foot of couloir above a rockband extending from the main NW face. This couloir (large bergschrund possible) is a plain snow/ice bed of 350m at $40/45^{\circ}$, finishing just L of pt.3639. The entry section may consist of rock exposures and the exit section closely corresponds with part of the normal W ridge route. In good conditions, AD, 4 h from foot of face. J.C. Poulin, J.N. Roche, 27 December 1972. All ways on this face are best done in the interests of security before end June.

CIME DES PLANETTES 2976m

POINTE DE L'OBSERVATOIRE 3015m

3534W. The 2 principal pts. on a rock spine running N from the Pte. de l'Echelle, the W side of which faces the Péclet-Polset hut across the upper Chavière valley. Rock generally good; several fine climbs have been made on this W flank since 1970. Approach from hut as for

R.131, leaving the Masse moraine to cross a prominent terrace N under large hummock 2639m and so passing below W side of both peaks (1½h).

137 <u>Planettes W face</u>. Start at lowest pt, just R of a gully cutting up lower part of slabby face. Ascend direct to rather more than mid height, then trend L in summit line between overlapping slabs; 400m, IV+, pegs. <u>NW pillar</u>. Start L of gully above lowest pt. and climb broad pillar along a wide corniche formed by the slabby W face and the overhung N facet; variable pitches, 350m, IV/V, pegs.

138 <u>Observatoire WNW ridge</u>. Already classic and popular, 400m, IV. The broad ridge base constitutes an independent buttress; a moraine rib runs out from the L (N) corner. Ascend round corner on N side (snow) for 5min. then go up loose blocky flank to reach crest of buttress above its initial step. Pleasant slabby steps on R side of crest lead to level top of buttress, and descend to gap beyond (II, bits of III). Traverse R to a chimney/crack system and climb this (III) to exit L near the crest. Now continue just R of crest by a succession of steep slabs (III/IV), latterly on crest itself, turning a gendarme R over loose blocks, to a rockhead and gap below (III/IV, var. pegs in place). From gap a groove L (III+) gives access to steep summit slab on R. Ascend this diagonally R across a cracked slab (IV, pegs), cross a groove and climb direct, trending L to top (IV, pegs) (3½h). There are shorter but more difficult routes on the SW face.

Descent: Follow small track/cairns along NE ridge in blocks then bear R (E) down scree to the adjoining Col d'Aussois (2916m) (15min.). Go down trail on N side (snow patches) for a few min. In the L (W) enclosing ridge is a saddle (2741m). Traverse this in a few more min. and go down steep broken rock and scree/snow W to the rough ground at foot of the WNW ridge (1h from summit).

AIGUILLE DU FRUIT 3051m

3533W, 3534W. Isolated, jagged rock mass; terrible rock and stone fall is a constant hazard. Superb regional view. A. Bermont, G. Tresallet, 1886 (W face couloir). Miss I. Marshall with L. Gromier and A. Ruffier, 1908.

139 <u>East Face Couloir and South-East Ridge</u>. The only recommendable way, safe enough from stonefall after mid July when all traces of snow have gone. Rock needs care, II. R.du Verger with J. Gromier, 23 August 1903. From the Lacs Merlet hut (R.56) follow path in cwm bed W and leave it just below upper lake. Go up grass and stone slopes S to a moraine terrace (c.2570m) overlooking lake. Above, 4 couloirs cut the E side of the mountain. Climb the 2nd of these from L, going

up scree tips cut by several rock steps; these are turned easily to reach the ridge at a gap – the 2nd in the crest coming from the summit ($2\frac{1}{2}$ h). Go up ridge on its R (E) side, using a chimney parallel with crest line above. In the top part of this steep crumbly chimney turn a large chockstone by the loose L wall. Emerge at a gap below the short summit step. Climb this to a block, surmounted by a steep slab on the L with small but good holds (30 min., 3 h from hut).

DENTS DE LA PORTETTA

3533W. A fretwork of limestone towers and gashes on the W side of the Chavière valley opposite Pralognan. See R.107,116. The approaches take at least 3 h, a lot of the rock is poor and the climbs are only between 100-200m long – although mostly very difficult. The E face of the Mey (2845m) was done (III) as long ago as 1924, but all the modern routes on this summit and the pinnacled tops N of this pt. date after 1970.

PETITE AIGUILLE DE L'ARCELIN 2648m

3533E. Lower W end of massive rock rampart enclosing N side of the Cirque du Dard; this inner (S) wall forms a long band, 250m high in places, petering out under the Gde. Arcelin (2759m) and adjoining the Col de l'Arcelin (2731m); the outer walls, W and N, average 500m. The easier routes are quite loose.

140 <u>West-South-West Ridge</u>. The pinnacle-like butt end of the Arcelin ridge. Notable, frequented rock climb in the Pralognan district, dolomitic in character, compact schist and limestone, mossy in parts, slippery and dangerous in damp conditions. 300m, IV+. R. Jeangeorges, R. Leininger, G. Tavernier, 7 September 1945. Approach as for R.117 to the narrow opening at pt.2236 into the Dard cirque. Leave the path, descend L across the stream bluffs and go up grassy rock shelves to foot of ridge ($1\frac{1}{2}$ h from carpark).

Climb 3 pitches by steep slabs and flake cracks, first on R side of crest, then on crest, then R again by a dièdre to ledge on crest (III, IV pegs). A wall L, the crest and a hard crack (V) lead in 3 further pitches to a shoulder. Just R again, cracked walls and slabs give 3 shorter pitches (III+/IV–, pegs) to near a steep step on crest. Climb this slightly R then direct to a little saddle (IV+). Now the more broken ridge above to the summit step. Traverse a few m R, climb a wall into a chimney and exit trending R up steep slabs to finish L on summit ridge (III+, IV, IV+, IV, var. pegs). The loose crest to top in a few min. ($3\frac{1}{4}$ h).

Descent: Follow crest E for 2 rope lengths to a vague gully on S side.

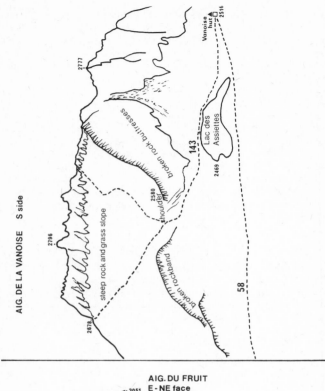

AIG. DE LA VANOISE S side

Vanoise hut 2516

Lac des Assiettes

2469

2777

2796

2678

broken rock buttresses

2580 shoulder

steep rock and grass slope

broken rockband

143

58

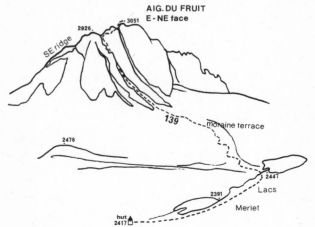

AIG. DU FRUIT E - NE face

SE ridge

2926 3051

139 moraine terrace

2476

2447 Lacs

2391 Merlet

hut 2417

Descend this for a rope length, then traverse L (facing out) along ramps and loose rock to descend the lower barrier further L; several pitches of II+. In the Dard bed, go down slabs, rubble and snow patches to the track of R.117 near foot of WSW ridge (1¼ h).

GRAND MARCHET 2651m

141   3533E. Huge limestone rampart towering above Pralognan. The terraced N face cliffs have been stormed by several difficult, somewhat dangerous, loose and unsatisfactory routes. Better climbs in the modern idiom are found on the NE ridge and its adjoining E flank pillars, facing the WSW ridge of the Petite Arcelin (R.140) on the outer rim of the Dard cirque. These routes of 300m are appreciably more difficult and delicate than the Arcelin ridge. The easiest way to the summit at the E end of its ridge lies directly above the Col du Gd. Marchet (R.117) by a conspicuous loose chimney L of the summit line (III), 45 min. from col to top.

ROC DE LA VALLETTE 2603m

142   3533E, 3634W. Another vast limestone wall facing NW above the Chavière valley, just S of Pralognan. A long narrow terrace cuts the face at 2/3rds height. Below this all the middle part of the wall has rather poor rock, but the lower slabs are good. Completion of the original route, resulting from several attempts by local guides, was achieved in 2 days by P.H. Biven, C. Fishwick, T. Peck, 26-27 August 1957; 550m, VI, A2. The line follows the L-hand side of slabs to the steep central wall under the terrace. Above that the climbing is open and easier. Another route made in 1967 starts c.100m further R and reaches a series of dièdres to finish R of the summit line; of similar difficulty.

AIGUILLE DE LA VANOISE 2796m

3533E. A knife edge with a long, nearly horizontal E-W crest. From either end (Vanoise hut or Pralognan) it looks like a gigantic pinnacle. The N face, above the Lac des Vaches, presents an impressive sombre curtain of smooth rock. There is an E top (2777m), forming a buttress above Lac Long. This modestly elevated rock fin is so accessible that it has become one of the most popular training scrambles in the Vanoise. First recorded ascent, 1911, though definitely climbed by chamois hunters before 1870. No written record of a British ascent before 1926 (Longland).

143   West-East Traverse. Those wishing to reach the top by the easiest way should ascend the descent part of the traverse, II. This outing is so popular that queues form along the ridge. Entertaining, good belays,

sound rock (though getting battered), very exposed for its grade, short pitches of II, several bits of III. Slightly easier in reverse direction; less than half a day's climbing. All the S side under the ridge is a steep grass slope broken by stones and slabby bands, technically easy but dangerous in damp conditions; rope up on it.

From the Vanoise hut (R.57) take a little track W and descend slightly to the Lac des Assiettes (2469m). Go round its N shore and climb the steep grass slopes above, faint track, to a shoulder (2580m). To the NW (L) go up through a break in the rock slab slope above and make a delicate traverse L over grassy rocks, aiming for the foot of the last step in the W end of the ridge; reach this at a small saddle (2678m) ($1\frac{1}{4}$ h). The step is steep and exposed with alternate walls and cracks. Climb it in 2 short pitches with good belays to a fine position overlooking N face. Now follow sharp pinnacled ridge with several layback or straddling movements to a walking section, then reach the highest pt. up its L side. Descend to a small gap and continue along crest without incident to a fine pinnacle; it can be avoided L by a ledge line or climbed over sensationally on good holds. The next part is narrow and exposed; pass over a 3rd pinnacle overhanging the N face. In a further 50m distance the ridge becomes easy (45 min.). Make a descending traverse R, down steep and rather smooth slabs, then grassy ledges S in order to reach the break through which the outward approach comes above pt. 2580 ($3-3\frac{1}{2}$ h for round trip).

North Face

An elongated boilerplate limestone wall above the Lac des Vaches, about 400m high and the most conspicuous landmark on the walk to the Vanoise hut (R.57). The foot of the face is reached in 20 min. from the causeway across the lake, about 1 h in descent from hut, or $2\frac{1}{4}$ h from Pralognan; $1\frac{1}{4}$ h from Bochor cableway.

Just R of the highest pt. a large squarish pillar marks the wall top. In the line of its L edge an angle divides the face vaguely into L (N) & R (NW) sections. The N part is crossed by a prominent black band, separating areas of grey rock at a slightly easier angle. In the summit line the band is distorted by a bulging nose before petering out at edge of the NW face. Above this nose a series of jutting, flat-fronted walls and flakes rise and converge towards the summit pillar; these features are defined L by a grey corner and R by a yellow corner. The upper NW face consists of a vertical wall merging into the summit pillar; its height reduces above a zone of overlapping slabs which further R overlook a couloir. A slabby rock knoll juts up into the base of the N wall just R of the overhanging nose and L of the angle with the NW face; this is the best pt. from which to identify the start of routes.

A dozen climbs of variable interest and quality can be noted but only one has become a classic, to the detriment of others equally good. Descriptions by the late Peter Biven of his early ascents cannot be traced exactly on the cliff. His 'direct' route does not correspond with the classic Bertrand-Desmaison and approximates more closely with the later Batel-Pasquier. His original ascent of the NW face, previously confused with the first (1955) ascent of the N face, seems to be ignored in French archives, and likewise cannot be traced precisely. The Biven routes are thought to lie in positions indicated on the diagram. Brief descriptions of routes are from his original reports. Selected important routes are as follows.

144 North Face Original. J. Bérard, R. Rigotti, 28 August 1955 (8 h). Starts at L side of face and takes cracked walls and slabs to an upper slabby zone at an easier angle, climbed diagonally R to summit ridge, reached at a pt. just E of the most easterly pinnacle. V.

145 Ollier-Pasquier. C. Ollier, M. Pasquier, 1963 (5 h). It starts just L of lowest pt., down to L of slabby knoll, and follows L side gutter beside bulging slabs to break out L to summit ridge. V+. A more difficult line (1967) runs parallel with this, VI.

146 Tomio. J. P. & R. Tomio, 1970 (6 h). Follows L side of the lower overhanging bulge, through the black band and continues a difficult line on overhanging slabs and walls L of R. 147. VI.

147 Bertrand-Desmaison. The classic route, climbed 10 times up to 1970 and often since then. The original start was much further R, coming out of the gully flanking the NW face and making a long traverse L to the overhanging R edge of the bulging nose. A direct start of no great difficulty is now used. Fairly clean with only a little loose rock. 18 pitches, 350m, V/V+, A1. All pegs normally in situ. A. Bertrand, R. Desmaison, 13 June 1964.

Start from top of knoll resting against face, best reached by steep loose rubble up its R side. A few m R, climb wall direct for 40m (III/IV), stance. Now traverse 40m L towards overhanging nose, stance. Here a vague dièdre cuts the overhangs. Climb a 4m wall, enter dièdre and climb it (V/V+, 7 pegs) to exit L at top, stance. Pendulum L to another lower ledge and follow it (III), stance. Now climb trending R up short walls (IV+/V, 2 pegs) towards a roof shaped like an inverted V; stance below it. Climb overhang at weakest pt., somewhat R, by a slanting crack (V, A1), stance. Traverse 3m L (V, peg) to foot of a dièdre; climb this to a ledge stance (IV+, 2 pegs). Continue up the next dièdre to another ledge (IV+, 3 pegs). Enter a third dièdre by traversing L (IV) and returning R up a tiny ledge line (V, A1, 6 pegs); ascend dièdre a short way to a stance. Now traverse 12m R towards a large flake and surmount it on the L awkwardly (IV,V, 2 pegs/wedges),

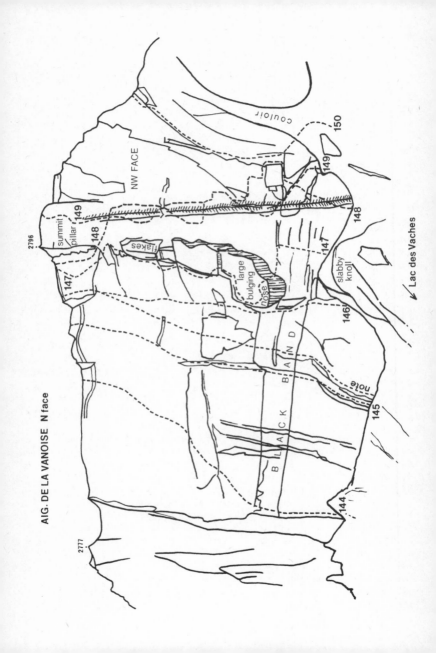

AIG. DE LA VANOISE N face

2796

summit pillar

NW FACE

flakes

large bulging nose

147

148

149

149

150

couloir

148

147

146

slabby knoll

145

note

144

BLACK BAND

2777

← Lac des Vaches

then go up a few m (III) to stance on R. Continue trending R towards the summit pillar for 50m (III); stance below a vertical wall. Turn wall R, going up large loose blocks (IV, peg) to a stance. Return diagonally L above wall, moving away from the corner marking the L edge of the summit pillar; so reach a stance. Continue trending L for 2 pitches (III, IV) (5-7 h).

148 Biven Route. See introductory remarks. It appears to start at the angle of the N and NW faces, down to R of knoll below R.147 but not as far R as the original start of latter. V+/VI, A1. P.H. Biven, T. Peck, 11 August 1964.

Climb slabs trending R for 45m (V), then straight up more broken rock for 30m (IV), to a short square tower overlooking gully on R. Avoid tower by horizontal traverse R into gully bed, then climb direct over loose blocks to a good ledge (IV). Climb a difficult crack for 12m (3 pegs), then move L to rib on edge of N face. The wall above with a series of hard moves (V, pegs) for 30m to a conspicuous yellow overhang. Ignore peg line up overhang (false route, evidently scene of an early attempt to make route completed by Batel-Pasquier); make a difficult and exposed traverse R over V grooves in the NW face, then climb a wall to a good ledge (25m, V). Move back L to a corner, climb it for 12m, then traverse horizontally L for 10m to another ledge (VI). Either climb the overhanging crack above or swing L with difficulty to reach a belt of slabs at an easier angle, leading up L to foot of the summit pillar. 3 easier pitches of V and a short traverse L on undercut holds lead to a wide chimney (wedges) under the yellow corner (V). Climb chimney, more broken rock which follows, then traverse 30m L to reach the L side of the pillar. Above is the final corner, about 90m, steep but not too difficult (IV, bits of V), some loose rock; finish up steep cracks to summit (12 h).

149 Batel-Pasquier. A. Batel, M. Pasquier, 31 July-1 August 1966. Pursues a relentless line up the angle dividing the N and NW faces. Much harder than R.147, 148 and had been tried several times previously. In the middle and upper part the Biven route appears to cross it twice in avoiding the major artificial pitches; it finishes up the dièdre corner cutting the front of the summit pillar. VI-, A3, 21 h.

150 North-West Face. See introductory remarks. The climb appears to end at the saddle (2678m) where the W-E traverse commences. Runs up a belt of overlapping grey slabs, very open and dependent on friction; long run-outs and small stances. 325m, V. P.H. Biven, T. Peck, 22 August 1957.

Start at foot of gully above a rock island and climb broken rock just L of gully for 90m. 2 pitches of 25m follow on open slabs of clean rock

Pte. Mathews, the Vanoise snowfield with the Dent Parrachée on the L, and the Péclet-Polset massif on the R, seen from the Gde. Casse.

(IV). Move into a corner above and layback/bridge for 50m to a small stance (V). Now follow L edge of slabs where they butt into vertical walls above; 3 good pitches of 30m to a small overhang. Above this the rock changes and needs careful handling for the last 30m (5½ h).

VANOISE (CHASSEFORÊT) SNOWFIELD

An elongated dome-like snow/ice roof, the second largest of its kind in the Alps, stretching N from the Dt. Parrachée to the Vanoise col. It forms numerous summits along its hogsback and at the edges, most of which are climbed frequently on foot or ski in spring and summer. As there are no lifts to any pt. on the snowfield, ski mountaineering is the welcome order of the day. Crevasses are normally not a serious obstacle but all the usual precautions should be taken. The chief summit caps are without exception superb viewpoints. The complete traverse, preferably from S to N, ranks among the best gl. touring expeditions of its class in the Alps.

POINTE DE LA RECHASSE 3212m

151 3533E. West Ridge. Rocky escarpment at N end of the Vanoise snowfield, opposite the Gde. Casse, visited by all and sundry. Agreeable regional view, F. From the Vanoise hut (R.57) cross a small grass and mud plain SW (track) and turn the E end of a rock barrier. The poor track trends L and ascends obliquely SE over rounded rocks and grassy terraces to black shale. At the top of this (snow patches) reach the edge of the Rechasse gl. at a spit of ground near pt. 2930 (1 h). Cross the barely sloping gl. SSW and attain the caudal end of the W ridge at pt. 3044. Go along R (S) side of ridge over a rock slope to join crest at a gap (3142m). This gap can also be reached from the N side directly across the gl. Continue on the broad crest, turning obstacles R. The last bit consists of small flat-topped towers of pavement hard stratified rock and leads to a madonna and cairn (1¼ h, 2¼ h from hut).

POINTE DU DARD 3206m

MONT PELVE 3261m

152 Better viewpoints than the Rechasse, easily reached as diversions of 25-40 min. from the Col du Dard (R.153), F.

DÔME DE CHASSEFORÊT 3586m

3533E, 3634W. The most frequented summit of the Vanoise snowfield, but not the highest. Extensive panorama. Ascended by hunters about 1850. A. & P. Puiseux, C. Maingot, 1 September 1876. W.A.B.

DÔME DE CHASSEFORÊT E side R.154

Vanoise snowfield

Génépy

2871

3127

△ Arpont hut

GR5

Coolidge with C. Almer father & son, 30 July 1884.

153   From Vanoise hut (R.57). Longish gl. trek across undulating and smooth slopes only slightly crevassed if the best line is followed, but easily lost in cloud; crampons essential. Start early to avoid return in soft snow. As for R.151 to pt.3044 ($1\frac{1}{4}$ h). Continue SW across the almost level gl., turning a big trough on L, then along centre of vast snowfield to the imperceptible dip of the Col du Dard (3153m) ($1\frac{1}{4}$ h). Now almost due W to skirt round the Pte. W du Mt. Pelve, bearing L (S) by a crescent shaped ridge of snow/ice; variable crevasse complications possible. Leave ridge as soon as convenient to bear SW again, keeping W (R) of the Col du Pelve. Avoid the temptation to climb directly S towards the Dôme by steeper crevassed slopes. Keep SW (R) until the broad back of the snowfield is reached near the Dôme des Sonnailles, then follow it S to the Col de Chasseforêt (3507m). Veer away L from saddle to reach broad W ridge of Dôme and follow this without incident, finally by a few rocks in the snow, to summit ($2\frac{1}{4}$ h, $4\frac{3}{4}$ h from hut, 3h in descent). F.

154   From Arpont hut (R.79). A circuitous, less steep and slightly crevassed way goes up the R side of the Ile torrent and the R (N) side of the Arpont gl. due W to its middle plateau, then N more steeply to the plateau slopes of the Chasseforêt saddle beside the summit ridge F ($3\frac{3}{4}$ h). More direct and interesting, by the E ridge gl. slope with reasonable regular steepness. Behind the hut follow a grassy rib NW, then a rocky depression to a tedious stony headslope N, trending L at top to R end of a barrier (2871m). Make a rising traverse over rough ground (snow) WNW to edge of gl. under E ridge. Climb gl. direct to broad ridge line, and follow this keeping L to avoid impinging crevasses. The ridge merges into rock which leads directly to the summit (4h from hut). F+.

155   From Vallette hut (R.73) a track SE goes past the old Lacs hut ruins and a pond to scree slopes adjoining the Col des Thurges. Bear L (ENE) over stony slopes to a long snow tongue coming down NW from the Sonnailles gl. Climb this directly with rock islands to rocks just behind (S of) the shoulder of the Dôme des Sonnailles (3361m) where, by a short snow gable R.153 is reached below the Chasseforêt col (hut to summit, 4h).

DÔME DES NANTS   3570m

DÔME DE L'ARPONT   3599m

3533E, 3634W. Nearly always visited in combination with attaining the Dôme de Chasseforêt. P. Puiseux, L. Boutan, 20 August 1877.

156   From the Chasseforêt summit or col an almost flat slope leads SW
to the Nants (30 min.). For the Arpont descend a snow slope S in a
few min. to the Col de l'Arpont (3503m), then ascend ridge ahead –
broad and easy with rocks on L – to the Arpont top (30 min.), F.

157   From the Génépy hut (R.72), quite steep and rough. Return to
the approach track and go up it to the foot of the last zigzags near pt.
2352. Now ascend L of the streambed due E to a moraine, followed
up E to a rockband. Turn this L (N) and return R to snow at N edge
of the Génépy gl. Ascend edge, trending L to an unpleasant snowy
rock slope mounting NE to a small gl. tongue fringing the Nants summit. Reach this trending R then L over snow, or by moving R all the
way; so cross the adjacent Col de l'Arpont to attain the Arpont top
($4\frac{1}{2}$h from hut), F+. Note: the classic route along the prominent
Génépy gl. terrace from S to N is generally badly crevassed after mid
July, PD.

DÔMES / POINTE DU GÉNÉPY   3576m

ARÊTE DE LABBY   3551m

158   3634W. A single ridge above the contiguous gls, stretching from
the Dôme de l'Arpont to the Pte. de Labby (3521m), quite narrow and
consisting of numerous rickety rock teeth separated by sharp snow crests
(cornices). Traverse, PD, pitches of II/II+, 3h.

159   Vanoise snowfield traverse S-N. It is not normal to include the
Labby-Génépy ridge (R.158); if this is done, add $2\frac{1}{2}$h. From the Dt.
Parrachée hut (R.78) a small track beside the water supply channel rises
N with marker cairns, passing close to hillocks 2645 and 2651, bearing
L above valley bed over terraces to return R to bed at pt.2860 under
the Génépy tarn. Follow a moraine N above W side of tarn and ascend
trending R to the Fond gl. Cross snowslopes due E to circle back L(N)
and climb a rockband by rubble at its R side, so slanting L to reach the
Col de Labby (3328m) ($2\frac{3}{4}$h).

From this col, by SE ridge to Pte.de Labby (3521m), keeping a little
on R side of crest, $1\frac{1}{4}$h, F. Splendid viewpoint.

From the col descend a little on to the Mahure gl. then ascend under
the Labby SE ridge to below the E facet of the Pte. de Labby. Now
traverse the gl. N, slightly downwards and under the Rosoire col, then
horizontally over moderately steep slopes with crevassed bulges often
in the same line, keeping roughly to c.3350m. Pursue this line N to
cross a steep shoulder under Génépy pt.3576, where a descent is necessary to reach the last crevassed part under the E side of the Col de
l'Arpont; ascend to latter by a moderate slope, then up to the Arpont

GRANDE CASSE   **Pte. Mathews**

R.160

All the route is visible, from the curving lateral moraine in the centre, on to the L side of the Grands Couloirs glacier, then up its centre with the 'grande pente' half in shadow, to the upper plateau and the summit ridge on L.

or Nants tops as desired (1¾h). This section, PD. Complete traverse to the Vanoise hut by reversing R.156, 153 (4h, 8½h in all without halts and in good conditions).

GRANDE CASSE 3855m

3533E. Crowning peak of the region, visible from afar in France and Switzerland. The panorama from the summit is exceptionally fine and extends from Monte Rosa to the Maritime Alps. Essentially a mountain climbed by snow/ice slopes, it displays an equal amount of rock in thin stratified foldings, all of which is of atrocious quality; the long ENE ridge typifies this. W. Mathews with M.A. Croz, E. Favre, 8 August 1860.

160 <u>West-South-West Face</u>. The normal route, ascending the Grands Couloirs gl. to finish by the W ridge. Halfway up, the 'grande pente' is exposed to slight stonefall from the W ridge flank. A straightforward snow climb with good situations. The final ridge is sometimes encumbered with large masses of snow, when care is required. PD.

From Vanoise hut (R.57) cross the main trail on the Vanoise col and find a small track descending slightly at first then contouring NE and N above Lac Long. The track crosses the terminal moraine of the Gds. Couloirs gl. and finally zags up to the lateral moraine crest where a rough scramble (cairns) leads to L side of the gl. near its base (1¼h). Ascend E to the gl. centre at a moderate gradient, generally broken by crevasses, sometimes with thin snow cover over ice. A steeper crevassed bulge leads to a longer unbroken section, rising to the foot of a steep slope extending across the gl. –the grande pente (1¼h). Start in the middle, cross the bergschrund and climb the slope working slightly L until at 2/3rds height one is close to the W ridge flank (250m, 45°), above which stonefall danger recedes. Trend back R on a moderating slope and emerge on the upper plateau, big holes and crevasses (1¼h). Continue to near the saddle area of the Col des Gds.Couloirs, then slant L (NE) to reach the W ridge at any pt. after its rocky flank has petered out (45min.). Follow ridge, snowy, with occasional outcrops, getting narrower, to summit. The last 60m is studded with little towers, rather loose, along the top of the tremendous, exposed N face (30min, 5h from hut, 2¾h in descent).

From the saddle, Pte. Mathews (3783m) is easily reached in 30min. by a diversion S (cornice). An infrequented var. up the R side of the gl. by a 50° slope called Couloir Massimi leads to the SW ridge of the Pte. Mathews subsidiary top near its summit, AD.

161 <u>North-North-West Face</u>. The N side of the mountain is dominated by a huge rectangular gl. face. The R-hand edge is marked by a

rock rib originating at the Col de la Grande Casse (3096m) and rising to the W ridge at 3677m (near pt.3685). The slope just L of this rock edge provides a classic snow/ice climb, AD. A. & P. Puiseux and A. Crochet with J. Amiez, 5 August 1887. H. Raeburn, C.W. Walker, 1 August 1904.

From Vanoise hut (R.57) cross the main trail on the Vanoise col to a track heading NE. This divides almost immediately; take the L fork, descending round the S end of Lac Long (2467m), then slanting N above the lake to reach the lateral moraine (2575m) of the Gde. Casse gl. Bear R, descending a little to the gl. and go up it NE over wide slopes, keeping R to avoid a few crevasses. Finally work up the centre to a bergschrund, usually closed, below a short slope leading to the Gde. Casse col; stonefall possible here ($2\frac{1}{2}$ h). From the col, reach on the L a steep little promontory covered with loose stones. Turn 2 gendarmes above it by moving L over an icy slope and rotten rocks (45 min.). Now move L onto the gl. face; ascend it directly then trend L, away from the bordering rib. At the foot of the steep upper slope cross a sometimes large bergschrund (or L), then go up the uniform upper slope at 45° to a level place on the W ridge ($2\frac{1}{4}$ h). Follow ridge to summit (45 min., $6\frac{1}{4}$ h from hut).

162 North Face (Italian Couloir). This ice curtain is marked centrally by a regular depression only vaguely resembling a couloir, which is closed at 2/3rds height by an ice bulge and séracs. In favourable conditions the prospect of falling ice from this zone is slight and the route passes L of it. Further L the face is bordered by the 'famously detestable rock' of the N spur. An ice climb often compared with Triolet N face and Gervasutti couloir in the Mt. Blanc range, but now rated easier than the TD standard. An elegant line, exposed, sustained, fine outlook all the way up. 700m, D+/TD-, average angle 53°, pitches of 60° possible. L. Binaghi, A. Bonacossa, 6 August 1933. J.R. Irons, P.L. Jones, 1969. Climbed 5 times up to 1955 and frequently since then. In good conditions, often climbed in 3h; one solo in $1\frac{1}{4}$ h.

Approach as for R.161. Descend from the Gde. Casse col (bergschrund possible) over plain snow slopes under the face, keeping R, till beyond the last of the lower rock outcrops surmounted by ice walls, an avalanche cone is reached (3h). At the top of this (bergschrund) climb an ice runnel then go straight up the L flank of the depression, at first alongside brittle rock L, variable; higher up the slope may be cut by slits, usually avoidable. Then slightly L in a continuously steep gutter to turn the main sérac band. An easier slope above it R can be followed before trending L again to approach a vague rib. Either climb the latter or stay on the ice slope, to continue by an ice rib merging into a hollow bordered L by a short rock spur coming down from the W ridge not far from

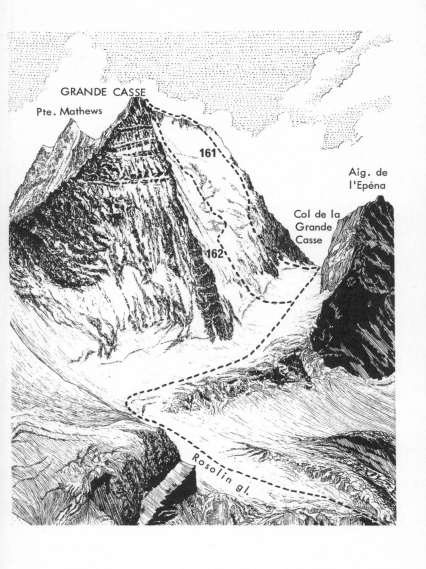

the summit. Skirt the spur R and continue direct to finish usually by 20m
of delicate rocks, landing on the ridge 10 min. from the summit (4-6h,
7-9h from hut).

AIGUILLE DE L'EPÉNA   3421m

POINTES DE L'EPÉNA   3348m   3307m   3293m   3264m

163   3533E. Elephantine rock rampart above the Gde. Casse gl. and
col. Easily the most mysterious and least visited major rock mountain in
the Vanoise park. While several unsatisfactory and artificially equipped
routes of no particular difficulty (badly exposed to stonefall) have been
made on the S side, the awesome, slab-smooth N face, in places nearly
750m high, remained untouched until 1966 when a series of TD/ED lines
were pioneered. The rock is an odd mixture of compact schist, granite
and limestone, often brittle and shattered or incredibly smooth; some of
it is quite sound but much is very loose. The mountain is not recommended except to those with designs on the N face routes (documentation at
Pralognan guides' office). H. Mettrier with G. & J.A. Favre, S. Gromier, 17 July 1900 (SW face 'bolt/pegs' couloir of pt. 3421). C.F. Meade
with J. & J.A. Favre, 18 July 1902.

PETITE GLIÈRE   3322m

164   3533E. _West Face and North-West Ridge_. H. Dulong de Rosnay,
J. Janin with M. & S. Gromier, 1893. The lesser SE pt. of the twins,
climbed from time to time and worthwhile for peak baggers. From the
Vanoise hut (R.57) follow R.165 to c.200m distance short of the final
slope to the Glière col (3h). On the R a steep ledge line covered with
stones trends L in the W face. Cross a sometimes large bergschrund and
follow this line into a shallow couloir running all the way up to the NW
ridge, well above the col, which is reached just above a pinnacle. Go
up narrow and exposed ridge to summit (1h, 4h from hut), PD+.

Note: The obvious depression in the S face above the Gde. Casse gl.
gives a V+, A1, 400m climb on poor to fair rock.

GRANDE GLIÈRE   3392m

3533E. The shapely upright twin of red rock, very popular scramble in
summer, queues and litter in high season. Splendid situations and views.
W.A.B. Coolidge with C. Almer son, 27 August 1887.

165   _South-East Ridge_. Splendid little rock scramble on sound granite,
varied approach, interesting throughout, much used as a training climb.
F+ (II). From the Vanoise hut (R.57) follow R.161 to the Gde. Casse

The common approach to these 3 routes can be clearly traced via the blunt ridge above the Col des Schistes to pt. 3078 and mostly hidden upper part of the S Glière glacier below the Col de la Glière.

gl. Cross it, rising slightly over moraine banks directly N to the other side, adjoining the Col des Schistes L. Ascend a ramp of schist/scree (track) to the col, 2845m (1¾h). Now climb a broad ridge N, at first on the crest with lots of holds, linked by grassy ledges, then if desired turn steeper obstructions in the upper part by scree ledges L; so reach pt.3078, a shoulder barely 15m. above the S Glière gl. Descend to gl. and cross the easy snow slope NE to foot of the Col de la Glière (3162m). An easy bergschrund and a short snow/rock slope lead to the col (1½h).

Go up a broad hump of scree/snow with large blocks to where the ridge steepens. The first buttress wall is climbed L by a chimney; the next and steeper either straight up on fine holds or by a flanking movement L. From a terrace, a third step is conveniently taken by another flanking move L. Rejoin the ridge R and follow to another steep section, turned by a chimney couloir L with good holds, to exit R near the top. Continue by the ridge, easing off to summit; scree terrace and large snow patch (1¼h, 4½h from hut).

166 West Ridge short variant. Very popular for a simple traverse of the mountain. Good rock and nice holds, PD, pitches of II+/III. H. Mettrier with S. & J. Gromier, 19 July 1901. As for R.165 to pt. 3078. On the Glière gl. cross to the opposite (N) side, under the SW face in the summit line. Go up broken rocks to an obvious chimney/couloir system slanting steeply L below the W ridge. Climb this on excellent rock, descending at one place to a snow patch to join a continuation of the line. Reach the ridge in a gap at foot of a gendarme in the form of a cube with a sharp point. Traverse L on scree to a smooth slab/wall split by an open chimney with an undercut base. Climb this with the aid of a chockstone and exit into a little gully which is climbed on the L to large blocks on the crest. Follow rock/snow crest to summit (4¾h from Vanoise hut).

Note: the complete ridge from the Br. du Gd. Gendarme (3148m) has pitches of III+/IV.

POINTE DU CREUX NOIR   3155m

3533E. Popular training rock and snow climb; various routes, mostly on good rock. E. Michelin, A. & P. Puiseux, 12 September 1884.

167 South-North Traverse. AD, numerous pitches of III. Descent, PD. R. Godefroy, 16 August 1918. From the Vanoise hut (R.57), approach by R.61, over the Col Rosset (2545m), and a short descent to foot of S facet of peak, supporting the bendy S ridge (1¼h). From near pt. 2512 cross to foot of facet and ascend lower part by a grassy gully. Soon

A Pt. 3385m R.168

C Pt. 3087m R.170

D Pt. 3378m R.168

E Pte. du Vallonnet R.168

F Pte. des Volnets

G Grande Glière R.165

H Petite Glière R.164

GRAND BEC

Becca Motta

Becquetta

Ptes. de l'Epena

Gde. Casse R.161 headslope

exit R and traverse R across steep grassy rocks split by gullies to reach the upper part of a narrow gully with chockstones. Ascend this with a through route under one block to emerge near R edge of facet. Follow L side of edge over broken slabs; turn a big slab R and climb a 2m chimney into a dièdre leading to a large smooth slab. Then a little ledge, like a track, awkwardly under an overhanging-bulging wall and on to a flake leading in a few m to a crack going up to scree on the S ridge proper. Go up the ridge, then follow a scree/snow ledge line on L (W) side, to a ridge gap also turned L; now climb steep rock with excellent holds, and a brow of mixed snow/rock to easier ground and scree/snow to a possible corniced exit at summit ($3\frac{1}{2}$ h, $4\frac{3}{4}$ h from hut).

Descent: Cross or turn the snowcap and follow crest (cornice) NE to forepeak 3154m. Here the ridge bends NNW. Go down snow to the lower part in shattered spiky rocks above the Col du Vallonnet (2997m). Quit ridge and descend R on steep snow into snow gully (called the Vallonnet gl. on map) on E side of col. Follow down, keeping L(N) in the lower trench to gain the mostly bare Patinoire gl. Go down this S to a track round W side of a tarn and so to the Gardes ch. (2431m) near the Lac des Vaches on the Vanoise hut approach route ($1\frac{1}{2}$ h in descent to lake).

Note: The descent is the usual ascent route. It can also be joined from the Grand Bec hut (R.59) by reversing the path into the Vuzelle cwm and ascending rough stony ground and snow patches to below the W side of the Col du Vallonnet. Climb the first couloir R (S) of the col; in its upper part work L onto a rib and take this to reach the N ridge about 50m above the col; then continue up ridge to forepeak and summit (hut to summit, $2\frac{1}{2}$ h).

GRAND BEC   3398m

3533E. Prominent roof-like snow and rock promontory with a gable end overlooking the Pralognan valley. Its comparative importance is underlined by 2 fairly recently constructed CAF huts. The rock varies considerably according to route.   A. Guyard with A. & J. Amiez, 19 September 1877. W.A.B. Coolidge with C. Almer son, 29 August 1887.

168   South-East Ridge. Fine mixed climb, more often used in descent after coming up the W ridge. PD, short pitches of II/II+. E. Bollard, R. Godefroy, 27 July 1900. From the Gd.Bec hut (R.59) cross the hut col and follow a few cairns up a steep grass slope E to stony ground mounting to the narrow Vuzelle gl. Climb this with increasing steepness, turning rock islands R and going up through narrows (40°) keeping L to reach by rocks a little snow saddle adjoining the Pte. du Vallonnet (3372m) ($2\frac{3}{4}$ h). The sharp ridge ahead is almost horizontal

GRAND BEC
NE side

Volnets

Vallonnet

3378

3385

R.168
SE ridge

R.170
rib

Becquetta

Becca
i Motta

R.170

and studded with little towers. Climb over or turn these on either side, but usually on the R (N), all on good rock, to junction with NNE rib (3385m). Continue along snow crest part of ridge, over a small saddle and some rocks, narrowing again (cornice) to the summit ($1\frac{1}{2}$ h, $4\frac{1}{4}$ h from hut).

169 West Ridge. The shortest way to summit; some poor rock. PD+, pitches of III/III+. H. Mettrier with J.A. Favre, S. Gromier, 11 July 1901. From the Grand Bec hut start as for R.168. At the top of the grass slope bear L through large blocks and snow patches to below a long rockband lying below S side of W ridge. Above and R of pt.2638, climb an obvious gully in this band to the scree and snowfield above, which in turn stretches R (E) under the W ridge. Ascend this diagonally NE to finish up a gully in the ridge flank at the crest a little way above gendarme pt.2908. Go up ridge on slabby rock either on the crest or turning gaps/obstructions on L side, until a large gendarme is reached. Move R and traverse into a gully system (ice) which is climbed to join gap behind the gendarme; one smooth slab pitch (verglas possible). Now move to L side of ridge into a gully system which is followed back to crest above all difficulties. Continue on crest to the summit ($3\frac{3}{4}$ h from hut).

170 North-North-East Rib (Pt.3385). Now the usual northern route, fine but variable snow climb according to season and conditions. PD/ PD+. E. Rochat with A. & J. Amiez, 25 August 1879. From the Plan des Gouilles hut (R.53) ascend track on grassy rib SE to stony ground rising under the Becca Motta to a snowfield called Becca Motta gl., then go into obvious Becquetta saddle ahead (2828m) ($1\frac{1}{2}$ h). In the same direction descend slightly across a terrace band near the bottom of the Troquairou gl., then climb L side of gl. on to snowy lower part of NNE rib, above its initial rocks. This rib is really a sub-wall supporting the gl. and dividing it from the much larger Volnets gl. Climb the rib line, sometimes on rocks but mostly further R on snow, quite pleasantly, with 2 or 3 possible crevasse interruptions, to the top at pt.3385 where the SE ridge (R.168) is joined and followed to the summit. Alternatively, and finer snow/ice work, climb the gl. itself in zigzags, according to crevasse disposition and steeper bands, direct to summit ($2\frac{1}{4}$ h, $3\frac{3}{4}$ h from hut).

GRANDE MOTTE 3653m

3533E. Graceful snow peak but one of the most defaced mountains of its elevation and relative prominence in the Alps. The reasoning that it offers no attractive climbing, and merely good summer gl. skiing, is defeated by the excellence of its ordinary routes which are first-class

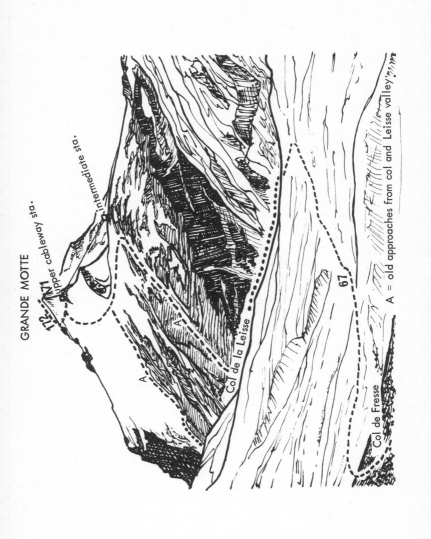

GRANDE MOTTE

172 171 upper cableway sta.

intermediate sta.

Col de la Leisse

67

Col de Fresse

A = old approaches from col and Leisse valley

snow trundles, not without danger, in the classic mould. The upper 250m on all sides consist of narrow, probably corniced ridges, prone to avalanche conditions. Magnificent viewpoint. T. Blanford, P. Cuthbert, E.P. Rowsell with J.A. Favret, 5 August 1864.

171 North-East (Cableway) Ridge. Though little more than 200m this upper ridge is often icy and the rocks verglassed. Not really recommended. In good conditions, rare, PD+. Normally AD/AD+. From the top station climb a short triangular snow/ice slope and move R steeply on snowy rocks to ridge apex. Follow crest delicately, with short movements L on poor rock (verglas), and sharp snow crests, to an easing off 50m below the snow crest summit (cornice) (1-2h). P. Puiseux, L. Boutan, 25 August 1877.

172 Normal Route from Cableway. F+. Straightforward though often with soft loose snow, and overlooking the Oxford Circus ski playground. It joins the original way from the Col de la Leisse. The latter gl. ascent is now not recommended because of constant large numbers of skiers on prepared gl. pistes. From the cableway (3450m) traverse horizontally S above the ski piste upper terrace in the gl. and after 5 min. make a rising traverse towards the long, obvious bergschrund under the E ridge. In the summit line this can be quite wide and steep; the further L you go, the easier it is. So cross it as soon as possible and climb the ridge flank to the E ridge crest, reached preferably above the last small outcrop step. Follow ridge pleasantly (cornice possible) to a steeper finish at the summit ($1\frac{1}{2}$h).

173 From South. The only route by which skiers can be avoided, but rather tedious, with interest in the upper half. F+. W.A.B. Coolidge, F. Gardiner with C. & R. Almer, 3 August 1889. From the Leisse hut (R.65) make a slightly rising traverse over grass, rocks and generally rough ground W on the N side slopes of the valley. After crossing a streambed, one km distance from hut, ascend more steeply on grass then stones to a little headland at c.2850m on a fairly prominent rib coming straight down from the Grande Motte signal cairn (3557m) high above. Climb this rib on loose broken rock, with several steep bits but no technical difficulty, to the upper section mixed with snow which in frozen conditions goes quickly to the flat signal headland ($3\frac{1}{4}$h). Now step on to snow and follow broad ridge ENE to finish up a quite narrow summit crest (30 min., $3\frac{3}{4}$h from hut).

SOMMET DE BELLECÔTE 3417m

3533E. Bucolic, attractive, outstanding viewpoint, rarely ascended before the PNV and La Plagne cableway developments; because of these, no longer a long trudge approach. The gl. slopes are notably on the S and W sides, while the N face is a complex tottering rock

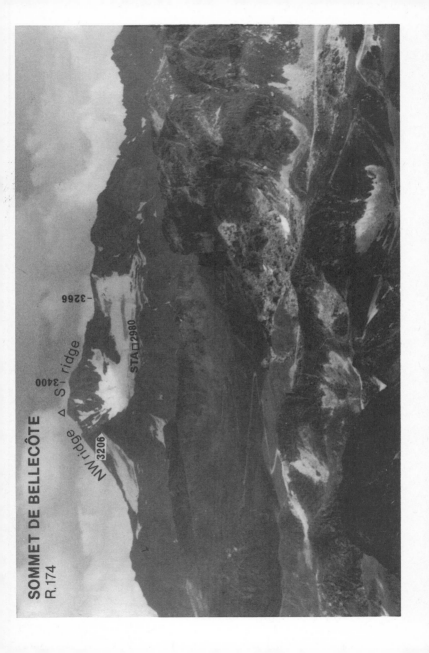

SOMMET DE BELLECÔTE
R.174

NW ridge 3206

△ S - ridge 3400

-3266

STA □ 2980

wall. All the rock is poor but this is not important on most routes.
R.C. Nichols, E.P. Rowsell with J.V. Favret, J. Tairraz, 12 September 1867.

174 From South by Cableway, Glacier and South Ridge; or North-West Ridge variant. Now the shortest ways with a choice of routes. The La Plagne – Roche de Mio – Bellecôte cableway is taken to the top sta. at 2980m at the foot of the Chiaupe gl. on W side of mountain. F/F+. Glacier route: Ascend diagonally R and go up beside the Chiaupe skitow to a short steep slope under rock saddle 3266m in the S ridge. Reach this saddle by a rather smooth ramp and large blocks (fixed cable). On the other side descend broken rock diagonally L (NE) to the Cul du Nant gl. Initially with a few crevasses, ascend the plain snow slope NE to saddle slightly R and close to the Dôme de Bellecôte (3381m); traditionally take 5 min. to move R (E) along its pleasant crest; splendid position above the Peisey valley. Return along crest, over saddle and traverse horizontally under last part of snow ridge to rocks L of the summit line; sometimes thin snow on ice here. Step off snow on to steep earth and broken rock, in which a poor slithery track goes up R in a few min. to summit (2¼ h).

South ridge, sound rock. As for previous approach to saddle 3266m. Now climb ridge, first up a step of large blocks (move R) then along crest with a few little obstacles turned R, to a steeper part taken nicely near the crest to a forepeak (3400m). Continue pleasantly to summit (1¾ h from cableway).

North-West ridge, normally used in ascent for making a simple traverse by coming down either of the previous ways. From the cableway walk out NE over snow and rock in the line of a skitow called the Traversée, passing under the triangular end of a spur coming off the NW ridge. This skitow leads to the narrow Bellecôte gl. Ascend this briefly SE to a notch in the spur at pt.3206. Now climb spur on its crest to junction with NW ridge proper. Go over or turn on the R (SW) side a number of little gaps and teeth and finish straight up a steep bit of ridge to the level summit area (2 h from cableway).

175 From South (Plaisance hut). The best approach from the Champagny valley. Recommended training climb, F+. Follow path beyond hut (R.49) for a few min. to near br. at pt.2184. Leave path, keep L (cairns) and go N to join the Plaisance stream. Ascend steep grass on its L side to an easement below and NE of the Pte. des Chardes. Now cross the stream and work up N over stones and moraine to reach the Cul du Nant gl. The lower tongue is normally steep and icy and it may be more easily mounted further R. Ascend it slanting L into the centre and go up the middle of the gl. with a few crevasses to join eventually R.174 coming from saddle 3266. Hut to summit, 4½ h.

L'ALIET   3109m

176   3533E. Assertive conical limestone peak standing between head
of the Peisey valley and the Bellecôte massif. Since the era of the
park, now much in vogue while previously virtually ignored. Smooth
slate-like rock, not entirely sound. Details of the numerous technical
climbs at Rosuel hut. H. Mettrier with J. Roux, 13 August 1904.

AIGUILLE ROUGE   3227m

177   3533E. Most northerly outlier of the Pourri massif. Fine regional
viewpoint,   reached on W side by chairlift and cableway from the Arc
2000 station. Local climbers have made rock routes on its flanks. From
a skiers' hut on the Gd. Col (2935m) the S ridge can be followed over
the Pte. des Arandelières (3178m) on mainly poor rock, avoiding easily
numerous small teeth and gaps with no technical difficulty, F+, $1\frac{1}{2}$h.
A. & P. Puiseux, L. Boutan, 8 August 1879.

AIGUILLE DU ST. ESPRIT   3419m

178   3533E. Outlier of Mt. Pourri, skirted by normal route to latter.
Its S face pillars give several stiff climbs on reasonable rock. The easiest route is from the Gd. Col (2935m) by N ridge, F, Pourri hut to
summit, $3\frac{1}{4}$h.

MONT TURIA   3650m

179   3533E. Caudal N end of Mt. Pourri proper, regarded among
alpinists as a separate summit. Good routes of no great difficulty cross
its summit to the parent peak (see below). The N face, going up the
E branch of the Grand Col gl., is a partcularly fine snow climb of AD
standard, at 45-50° with no special complications or hazards; E. Rochat
with J.J. Blanc, V. Mangard, 13 August 1880 (start from Turia hut).
Mt. Turia first traversed by Miss M.C. Brevoort, W.A.B. Coolidge
with C. Almer sr. and 2 porters, 2 July 1874.

MONT POURRI   3779m

3533E. Culminating pt. of a mini-range streaming with gl. on all sides,
and extending N-S for 6km from the Gd. Col to the Col de la Sache.
Most of the climbing is moderately to fairly difficult, and snow/ice
problems predominate; all of it requires a degree of experience of high
mountain terrain. The complete traverse of the main ridge is the finest
expedition of its class in the Tarentaise. Following an ascent of the
Dôme de la Sache outlier by W. Mathews, F.W. Jacomb with J.B. &

M.A. Croz, 15 August 1861, Mathews suggested that Michel Croz might attempt the principal peak on his own later in the season. Thus the first ascent was accomplished by the famous Chamonix guide, solo, 4 October 1861. The climb was repeated by W. Mathews, T.G. Bonney with J.B. & M.A. Croz, 5 August 1862. The first traverse of the main N-S ridge was made, in the reverse direction, by E. Rochat with J.J. Blanc, V. Mangard, 13 August 1880.

180   Geay Glacier Normal Route. Classic Vanoise snow/ice climb, serious, PD+/AD. W.A.B. Coolidge with C. Almer father & son, 8 August 1878. From the Mt. Pourri hut (R.41) to old Regaud hut in 30 min. (R.42). Note there is a vague track after 10 min., cutting across slopes E to gain the long Geay moraine some way above Regaud; saves 20 min. Go up track NNE on moraine to below S side of Aig. du St. Esprit, and descend a little to N edge of the gl. Ascend E generally in the centre between crevassed bands/séracs, moving L higher up but depends on conditions; sections at 40-45°. Higher up skirt the gl. slopes below the ridge of the Col des Roches, and curve round S over crevassed slopes of the upper gl. plateau. Cross a normally large bergschrund (can be quite tricky/delicate in descent), probably best near L end, to climb the steep upper slope on the R (W) and reach the W ridge at its upper shoulder (c.3575m); splendid situation. Either climb the steep snow ridge to summit, or use rocks below it on R (S) side, in the same angle plane as the snow crest, 40-45° (5 h on average from the old Regaud hut; allow same time for descent).

181   Mont Turia and North Ridge. Excellent mixed climb, popular, serious, AD. W.A.B. Coolidge, Miss M.C. Brevoort with C. Almer sr. and 2 porters, 2 July 1874. As for R.180 to below the Col des Roches (3443m). Climb a short, steep snow/ice slope, then steep loose rock or similar gully R to this shoulder col on the NW ridge of Mt. Turia. Ascend L of crest on steep mixed ground, then similarly along upper edge of N face (R.179) to attain Mt. Turia (3650m) by a narrow rock crest (4¼ h). Go along crest of N ridge towards the summit, horizontal for some distance. After an easy mixed part, the crest is splintered with small teeth and gaps; some are crossed, others turned L. A tower larger than the rest can be climbed direct on reasonable rock; elsewhere some large loose blocks need care. As the crest steepens, snow crest sections appear, alternating with short rock steps (cornices possible); so reach the summit (1½ h, 5¾ h from old Regaud hut).

Note: Access to this route from the Turia hut (R.44), via the Turia gl., Col de la Gurraz (3169m) and NE ridge of Mt. Turia is likely to prove troublesome on upper part of the gl. section, just below the col (ice and other obstacles at 50°). More easily done by climbing the N face of Mt. Turia (R.179).

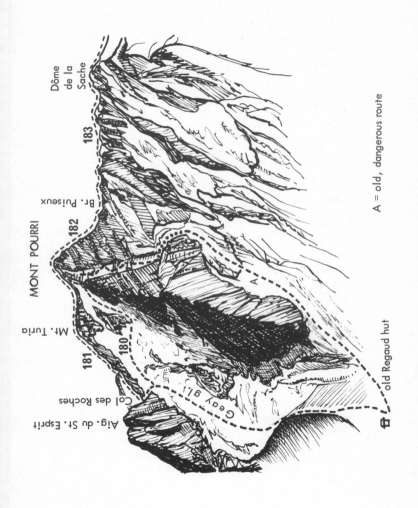

Dôme de la Sache

183

Br. Puiseux

182

MONT POURRI

Mt. Turia

181   180

Col des Roches

Aig. du St. Esprit

Glacier

A

old Regaud hut

A = old, dangerous route

182 **South Ridge (from East Side)**. The usual route when coming from Tignes/Val d'Isère. Crevassed gl. work and serious mixed terrain with fine positions, interesting. PD+. From the Martin hut (R.45) follow a path NW, away from the Pourri circuit trail, to traverse in rocks under the Savinaz gl. (2233-2289m). At the Savinaz stream the track starts to descend. Leave it and follow R side of stream W, and so ascend rocks and scree R to reach the front of the Rochers Vieux promontory. Bear L and ascend the broad hollow of this promontory SW to slabs and rock terraces below the S Gurraz gl. at an inlet 200m above and SW of pt. 2639 (1¾ h).

Walk out on to the moderate gl. slope and ascend it SW, turning several enormous crevasses and low ice walls as they are found. Continue in the same direction towards the wide saddle-depression of Br. Puiseux at foot of S ridge. Bear R of a rock projection in the gl. where there is a crevasse entanglement, cross a bergschrund – sometimes quite large at end of season, and climb a short but steep (45°) ice slope with a few rocks to the saddle (3469m); reach crest at R-hand end, close to rock face on R (2 h).

Follow the rocky crest, almost horizontal at first, then consistently steep, where in good conditions the narrow edge should be scrambled direct on firm rock. With verglas or fresh snow, use in turn the L and R flanks – loose ledges and chimneys; 2 pitches of II+ and one of III-. Reach a false summit (snowcap on rock) and continue usually by a snow crest to main summit (2 h, 5¾ h from the Martin hut).

183 **Main Ridge Traverse**. Traditionally, this splendid expedition is undertaken in the direction N–S, descending from the Dôme de la Sache, over the Dôme des Platières, and down to the Col de la Sache; this descent is very rough and tiring. Parties are recommended to go down to the Martin hut, and spend another day returning along the Mt. Pourri circuit trail. By R.181 to summit and down S ridge (R.182) in 1¼ h to Br. Puiseux (total, 7 h).

Section: Br. Puiseux – Dôme de la Sache. PD/PD+. Follow the undulating ridge of the saddle, crossing 3 outcrops quite easily. Now go up a short slope to where the ridge narrows (3533m). A rock ledge on the R can be used initially, then follow the narrow snow/ice crest to a gendarme, which is turned L. Continue along crest, over two rock humps, to a snow dome (3585m), which is crossed to the final snow/ice ridge slope leading to the Dôme de la Sache (3601m) (2 h, 9 h from the Mont Pourri hut).

Descend the E ridge on snow and rock for a few min. until it is possible to move L (N) easily down the broad gentle slopes of the Savinaz and Gurraz upper plateau. Long, large crevasses are usually easily turned with detours. Descend to join the gl. approach used by R.182; reverse this to the Rochers Vieux promontory, and so down to the Martin hut ($2\frac{1}{2}$h, $11\frac{1}{2}$h without halts). This descent is the usual route for climbing the Dôme de la Sache as an option for bad conditions on Mt. Pourri, F/F+ ($4\frac{3}{4}$h).

POINTE DE LA SANA   3436m

3533E. An isolated peak with long graceful ridges, giving it a symmetrical appearance on all sides. The rocks are extremely rotten; the NW face has interest as a snow/ice climb (D-) in early season when it should be free from serious stonefall. In spring, a classic Val d'Isère ski climb. P. Puiseux, L. Boutan, 18 August 1877. W.A.B. Coolidge with C. Almer son, 30 August 1886.

184   East Ridge/Sana snowfield. The normal route, F. From the Femma hut (R.68) follow the valley trail E for a few min., then take a line of cairns L, mounting NE past the Rocher Rond and near the R side of the Femma/Côtes streams. Work up N over pasture with bits of a track to a terrace area above stream crossing pt.2729. Bear L (NW) across this to mount stony slopes cut by low rockbands. Go up through these NW to the snowfield lying below the E ridge (called Sana gl. on the map), adjoining the Col des Barmes de l'Ours (3077m) ($2\frac{1}{4}$h). Ascend the L (outer) side of the snowfield, and finish R (N) by schist outcrops at the summit (1h, $3\frac{1}{4}$h from hut).

Note: The Val d'Isère summer approach co-incides with R.69, to the Pissets plateau pool. Here a track breaks off WNW for one km to pt. 2643. Now go up grassy moraines SW to the Barmes de l'Ours gl. Bear S up the gl., crevasses possible, to the Col des Barmes de l'Ours, from where the E ridge can be followed above the snowfield with a scramble over schists, rocks and snow patches (6h from Val d'Isère).

Spring skiers come from the Bellevarde lift systems. They can be towed now to the Col des Près, from where a 3 km traverse SSW via the park chalet near pt.2624 leads to the N end of the Barmes de l'Ours gl.

185   West-South-West (Charbonnier) Ridge. Nice scramble with sharp snow crests in early season, F+. P. Engelbach with C. Roderon, 13 August 1897. From the Leisse hut (R.65) descend from the main footpath, over a shoulder W, to cross the Leisse stream at its junction with the Charbonnier stream pt.2461. Now ascend grass and stones S to the L end of a terrace area and continue ascending SE round a stony spur, pt. 2719, and mounting this steeply to the upper W edge of the Leisse gl. At this pt. the gl. is a moderately inclined snowfield under the Pte.du Charbonnier. Ascend snow SE to saddle 3236 on the ridge ($2\frac{3}{4}$h). The ridge pleasantly over successive humps and saddles (cornices possible),

PTE. DE SANA

WSW ridge

3311

R.185 △ E ridge R.184

3411

3334

3238

3077 3147

PTE. DU MONTET R.197

Pisaillas gl.

AIG. PERS R.197

mostly on rock, to a steeper finish above the Leisse gl. face on your L
(1 h, 3¾ h from Leisse hut).

POINTE DE MÉAN MARTIN   3330m

3633E. Popular training ground with a variety of easy snow and mixed
routes, and a pretentious mini N face. Splendid viewpoint. P. Devot
with M. Folliguet, G. Brun, 6 August 1877. W.A.B. Coolidge with
C. Almer father & son, 18 August 1883.

186   North-West Ridge. Mixed ground, F/F+. From the Femma hut
reverse R.69 to the Rocheure col (2 h). Continue E/SE along the main
ridge to the Pte. du Pisset (3033m) and on the far side descend a few
rocks to the broad Col du Pisset (2958m) (30 min.). Now go up broad
ridge R of outcrop 3030m to a shoulder (3130m) at edge of the Fours gl.
Follow ridge in pleasant position on rock and snow to the terminal rock
pile (1½ h, 4 h from Femma hut).

From the Fond des Fours hut (R.70) follow a track on L (E) side of the
stream along the outfall bed on grass and stones to the frontal moraine
of the Fours gl. Keep R (W) along moraine and quit it to ascend with
cairns SW to a small snowfield between pt. 2970 and 3030. Go round
the far (W) side of latter pt. to join the approach from the Femma hut
(3½ h from Fours hut to summit).

187   East/North-East Ridge. Over the Signal de Méan Martin 3315m.
Popular traverse combination, F/F+. From the Fond des Fours hut, as
for approach to Fours gl. (above). On reaching the Fours gl. moraine
bear L (SSE) to the L edge of the gl. some 500m distance R of the obvious Col des Roches. Go up this moderately steep edge of the gl. to
a little saddle (3035m) on the NE ridge. Cross on to the Roches gl.
and ascend latter to avoid a rock step on the ridge. Return to the ridge
and go straight up (or R on Fours gl. again) to the Signal (2¾ h). Go
along main ridge W on rock and snow to principal summit (30 min., 3¼ h
from Fours hut).

188   North Face. The Fours gl. can be climbed according to conditions either directly to the Signal pt. or to the true summit. Slopes of
45°, normally AD, 350m. Used by parties under instruction.

GRAND ROC NOIR   3582m

189   3634W. Chiefly of interest to peak baggers; poor rock. French
army surveyors, 1864. W.A.B. Coolidge with C. Almer son, 27 August
1889. The shortest and most convenient approach starts from the Vallonbrun hut (R.86). Take R.120 to the Pierre aux Pieds (2½ h), then
continue NNW up a grassy rib and trend R higher up to the Diet stream.

Follow up its L side to moraines, stones and rockbands under the little Pisselerand gl. Work up its R side and at the top climb a steep snow/shale gully (loose) to a small shoulder under the large summit tower. In its SE face climb a chimney/gully to the top; awkward, loosely laminated rock pitch exit, PD ($2\frac{1}{2}$h, 5h from the Vallonbrun hut).

CENTRAL GRAIANS FRONTIER RIDGE

Described from N to S. Contrary to expectations, this section of the guide has been reduced in extent compared with the old Graians West guide. A number of problems arise with greatly expanded facilities on the Italian side of the range, adjoining the Gran Paradiso Park where the access to climbs, etc. is changing. For the present only the normal routes on the main peaks, and a number of other notes/observations, are included. The definitive guides for this zone are in the Italian CAI/TCI series: Alpi Graie Centrali (1985), Alpi Graie Meridionali (1980). Equivalent volumes in French are not published.

AIGUILLE DE LA GRANDE SASSIÉRE 3747m   3751m IGM

3633E. The superior height of this mountain attracts many ascents; on the other hand it offers rather poor climbing but the ordinary route is worthwhile for the magnificent summit panorama. Noted for the striking stratification of its immense S wall in terrible rock, about 1200m high. The Ital. side is covered by the large double Vaudet-Gliairetta gl. system. First ascent by an inhabitant of Tignes, about 1808. By a tourist: W. Mathews with M.A. Croz, 5 August 1860.

190 _West Ridge_. Ordinary route, a long ramble, F. Axe necessary. From the Saut ch. (R.90) follow road for 200m to paths on the L. Do not take the prominent traverse path L (W). A small track cuts straight up NNW to join another coming from the R, at the R end of a little broken rockband, and at the lower edge of the Plan de la Casette. Follow the track L (W and N) across this pasture area, then go up grass and stones NE (cairns) in order to approach the scarp edge below the W ridge at c.2900m. Turn several little barriers before reaching ridge which leads up more steeply, and finally by a few rock terraces covered with schist to a ridge junction at pt.3313. Here the upper plateau of the Sassière gl. overlaps the flat ridge; cornice on R (S) side possible. Keep L without losing height and follow snowy ridge edge to the foot of the final pyramid at c.3550m. The last snow slope is about 30° and leads rapidly to rocky summit and large cairn. In a dry season the

final pyramid becomes a shaly slope in which traces of a path are found (5 h from the Saut ch.).

LA TSANTELEINA 3602m 3601m IGM

3633E. The most attractive summit on the frontier ridge in the vicinity of Val d'Isère. It gives a number of excellent snow climbs. Tsanta = steep slope; Santel is a modern variation. T. Blanford, R.C. Nichols, E.P. Rowsell with J.V. Favret, R. Frasseron, 9 August 1865.

191 West Side (Santel Glacier). Though not quite the easiest way up the mountain this is the most pleasing, interesting and satisfying route. PD-/PD. Start not later than 5 am. From Val d'Isère, as for R.113 to the Col de la Bailletta (2852m) ($3\frac{1}{2}$-4 h). From here an opening to the NE will be noticed in the side of the Santel gl., which itself is not visible, to the R (E) of pt.3060. First, skirt along the base of the rock ridge to the E, then contour grassy terraces between long low rockbands to the NE and N, rising only after one has come below the big buttress on the R (S) side of the Santel gl. Go up easily across terraces and round large blocks into the opening, a level gateway onto the gl. above a lower crevassed tongue (1 h).

Climb the moderately inclined gl. near its R side, and later move to the centre (a few crevasses), going straight up to a steep section. Cross a bergschrund, generally without difficulty, and climb the slope rather on its L side for 150m at $40°$ until the W ridge above and L begins to look like an attractive proposition. By a simple traverse L reach ridge and follow the broad, rock studded crest, all sound and possibly plastered with snow/ice, to a false summit. Continue along a narrower mixed ridge to the summit; tin box for visiting cards (2 h, $6\frac{1}{2}$-7 h from Val d'Isère; $3\frac{1}{2}$ h in descent).

Notes: Starting from a camp (future hut site) near the Sassière lake dam (2461m) on NW side of the Bailletta col, the approach to the Santel gl. gateway is about $1\frac{1}{2}$ h shorter. From the same site, a longer approach to the N face above the Rhêmes-Golette gl. provides a fine snow/ice climb of 400m from near the Col de la Tsanteleina. On the Val d'Isère side of the mountain the Couart dessus gl. marginally gives the easiest route, approached as for the Santel gl., inasmuch as the snow slopes do not exceed 30-35°, but access to the Couart gl. is increasingly over steep and very bad moraine rubble.

POINTE DE BAZEL 3440m 3445m IGM

192 3633E. Ital: Punta Calabre. Unseen from Val d'Isère the long, prominent ESE wall of this mountain, adjoining the Col de Rhêmes-Calabre (3076m), has been developed since 1970 into a major rock

W ridge

TSANTELEINA Santel gl. R.191

climbing area, now with a dozen routes on compact limestone, about 400m high. The approach is from Pont St. Charles on the main road (R.28,91); there is hardly any advantage gained by starting from the Prariond hut. Climbing details available at Val d'Isère.

POINTE DE LA GALISE   3343m   3346m IGM

3633E. The panorama from this summit is generally considered to be one of the finest in the Alps. This is entirely due to the favourable position occupied by the mountain where its height is just sufficient to make the most of openings between big mountains on all sides. The peak is well seen from Val d'Isère – the most popular summer climb from this resort and the raison d'être for the Prariond hut. Recorded ascent: J. Heelis, G. Yeld with A. Payot, J. Martin, 17 August 1878 (though climbed at least 20 years prior to this date).

193 West Side (Bassagne Glacier). Very pleasant outing, F-. Axe necessary; crevasses possible. From the Prariond hut (R.91), for a few min. go up the splendid path E on the grass spur towards the Col de la Galise, to pt. 2499. Now fork L along a little track slanting up NE to cross the Niolet stream below pt. 2630. Ascend the stony slopes then moraines in the same direction (cairns), bits of track every where, bearing L (N) on old moraine to reach the Bassagne gl. just under the Col de Bassagne (3105m) ($2\frac{1}{2}$ h). Walk out onto the snow field and go up it due E near the frontier ridge, turning rock projection 3285m R to attain directly the small pyramid of rocks forming the summit (45 min., $3\frac{1}{4}$ h from hut).

Note: SW ridge, from the Col de la Galise (2987m). Often climbed to make a simple traverse; PD in lower part on poor rock with turning movements, short pitches of II+ (hut to col, 2 h, plus 2 h for ridge).

COL DE LA GALISE   2987m

194 3633E. The most important pass into Italy in this section of the frontier ridge; used by the local people for several centuries, from Val d'Isère to the Val d'Orco (Ceresole). A fork L (N) leads over the adjacent Colle del Nivolet (jeep road, hut, etc.) to Pont hamlet at the W foot of the Gran Paradiso – this being the easiest approach from France. On the Fr. side the pass is reached without difficulty from the Prariond hut (R.91) in 2 h. The Ital. side is at first in two steep earthy couloirs, quite loose, with fixed cables – tricky under snow and needing care from walkers; otherwise well marked and all straightforward.

GRANDE AIGUILLE ROUSSE 3482m

3633E. Splendid mixed excursion, popular, highly recommended and a magnificent viewpoint. Recorded ascent: E. Rochat with J.J.Blanc 31 July 1878. Probably climbed by hunters as early as 1820. W.A.B. Coolidge with C. Almer son, 31 August 1887.

195 Traverse by West and North Ridges. An attractive combination, F/F+, no technical difficulties but possibility of crevassed slopes that need care. From a little below the Prariond hut (R.91) cross the river plain S at pt.2296 where planks are placed (otherwise tricky crossing – go some way upstream and come back). Now ascend pleasant slopes on the L (E) side of the Gros Caval stream, and pass R of the Tête des Chèvres dome (2777m), through a scree trough to reach moraines of a branch gl. tongue coming down below and W of pt.3053. Ascend the gl. bowl on the L and continue directly to the Col du Montet (3185m) on the main W ridge (3 h). Climb a broad scree slope covered with large blocks on L of crest to pt.3343. At this pt. in the ridge there is a 30m vertical drop, over which one can abseil (in ascent, on excellent rock, IV+), but this is seldom done. About 50m before pt.3343 make a descending detour across a fairly steep snow/rock slope on the L (N), and so turn the obstacle; regain the ridge by easy slopes of the Sources de l'Isère gl. Continue along the easy crest to the Petite Aig. Rousse (3432m) (1¼ h). Descend the main ridge into a broad snowy depression (3368m). Go along a nice snow ridge, possibly corniced, and finally by some rocks to the chief summit (30 min., 4¾ h from hut).

From the summit descend the NE ridge to the Pas du Bouquetin (3335m), a junction of ridges at the Fr.-Ital. frontier rather than a natural pass. Go down L side of ridge (bad snow possible), then traverse two small gendarmes on the crest (3375m) before reaching the bottom; this ridge can be heavily corniced (30 min.). Continue down a pleasant snow/rock ridge to Col d'Oin (3164m) below the abrupt head of Cime d'Oin. Now descend gl. slopes W and NNW, avoiding a few big crevasses and coasting down parallel with the frontier ridge to near the Col de la Vache (2955m). Bear L (W) off the gl. over slabby rockbands to snowbeds and moraine terraces (cairns) where the good Isère Sources track is picked up and followed down to the Prariond hut (2 h, 2½ h from summit; round trip, 7¼ h without halts).

196 Traverse from Carro Hut (R.92). Equally popular but distinctly more difficult on the outward leg. PD/PD+. Follow a track NNW above the black tarn over grassy hummocks (cairns) and keep L when it bears R (NE) towards the Col du Carro. Go up the broad stony cwm bed NNW with boulders and snow patches and in the line of the stream coming from snow at the top. Ascend latter to prominent gully on the R,

rising to the Pas du Bouquetin. Climb the steep gully on snow, ice or rock, conditions vary, normally using run-out security, getting narrower and with stonefall possibility, to exit at ridge junction col on the R ($2\frac{1}{2}$ h). Now reverse R.195, going up the NE ridge, to summit (1 h, $3\frac{1}{2}$ h from Carro hut).

The descent follows the main ridge W (R.195) to saddle 3368. Descend the S side over easy rocks and snow to broken ground above a rockband. Keep 100m R (W) of the main drainage gully below, and go down the L side of a secondary gully in the barrier. Once below, scree leads down to the Gontière tarn (2956m). Descend its outfall (track) which becomes the Plan Sec stream to the Carro balcony path near pt. 2728. Go along this horizontally E, back to the hut, F (2 h, in ascent, 4 h. For round trip traverse without halts, $5\frac{1}{2}$ h).

POINTE DU MONTET 3428m

AIGUILLE PERS 3386m

197 3633E. This T-shaped arrangement of ridges between the neck of the Col de l'Iseran and the frontier ridge affords traditional training climbs. Due to the invasion of summer skiing, not much in vogue today. Various chairlifts and skitows start from near the new access road running NE from the col to near the base of the Col Pers couloir. As the latter gives access to the normal route via the easy W ridge to Aig. Pers, in summer the scrambler is liable to be knocked down by skiers. Routes off the easy Pisaillas gl. on to the easy N-S Montets ridge are prone to similar hazards. By riding to the top of the Cascade chairlift, the Pers and Montet tops can be climbed in $1\frac{1}{4}$ h.

LEVANNA OCCIDENTALE 3593m

LEVANNA CENTRALE 3619m

3633E. The principal objectives for climbers at the Carro hut (R.92). The main rock slab crest is altogether 3km long but mixed ground is the predominant feature, with good and bad rock. Occid: J.J. Cowell with J. Culet, M. Payot, 10 September 1860. Cent: L. Vaccarone, A. Gramaglia with A. & D. Castagneri, 17 August 1875. J. Heelis, G. Yeld with J. Martin, A. Payot, 12 August 1878.

198 Frontier Ridge Traverse. The ordinary route approach to the W summit is F, and many do not go beyond this pt.; very fine simple trip. The connecting ridge to the central top is loose and pinnacled, PD, but depending on snow conditions possibly delicate. The descent is the normal (separate) ascent route to the central top, PD-. From the Carro,

follow a track ESE beside the white tarn and go up a broad trench under the Col des Pariotes. Leave the main track (large cairn), break off L and follow cairns over rubble and blocks to the lower edge of the Derrière les Lacs gl. at pt. 3091. Ascend snowslope E and bear R (SE) up snowy rock to crest of W spur coming off the frontier ridge. Follow this on snow/rocks to where the ridges merge and take a narrower crest to the top ($3\frac{1}{4}$ h from hut).

From the W top the ridge running towards the Cent. top is narrow and rocky with linking snow crests, sometimes corniced. Turn successive groups of teeth on the R (S) side. The laminated rock is often loose, especially beyond the lowest ridge dip at the Pas de la Levanna, pt. 3509. Allow $1\frac{1}{2}$–2 h. From the Cent. top descend the S face directly over sloping terraces and banks of smooth rock, often snow covered, towards a large scree zone. Below this are further terraces separated by rock barriers. Finally go down a long scree shoulder SW which divides the tiny Trois Bec gl. and large Sources de l'Arc gl. Skirt R (NW) above the last rockband then turn down rough rocky slopes WSW, past the Arc sources pools, to reach the cairned Pariotes track. Follow this NW over the Grand Fond stream near pt. 2800 and ascend track to the Pariotes col (3034m) where the outward route is soon rejoined (Cent. top to hut in descent, 3 h. From W top, 5 h. Round trip without halts $8\frac{1}{4}$ h).

Note: A local classic rock climb is the ESE pillar/edge from the Pas de la Levannetta (3372m), $3\frac{1}{2}$–4 h approach from the Carro hut. Though short, has mainly good rock to top of pillar, 250m, IV+/V. Then by a stepped ridge with pitches of III/IV to Cent. top ($4\frac{1}{2}$–$5\frac{1}{2}$ h for technical climbing).

LEVANNA ORIENTALE   3556m

199   3633E. Double summit at S end of the Levanna ridge, visited infrequently. Long approach to Col Perdu (3285m) from Carro hut in 4 h, then up the N ridge in $1\frac{1}{2}$ h, PD–. Lord Wentworth with G. Blanchetti, 25 September 1874, by E ridge (cairn found on top).

MULINET RIDGE - ROC DU MULINET   3442m   3452m IGM

POINTE MEZZENILE   3436m   3429m IGM

3633E. The Roc du Mulinet is called Punta Martellot by the Italians. A serrated rock ridge of steps, towers and pinnacles, affording one of the best traverses of medium difficulty in the district. Mainly good rock but exposed and prone to verglas. A traverse S–N is AD, N–S is AD+. A consideration in choosing which direction to follow is that the descent

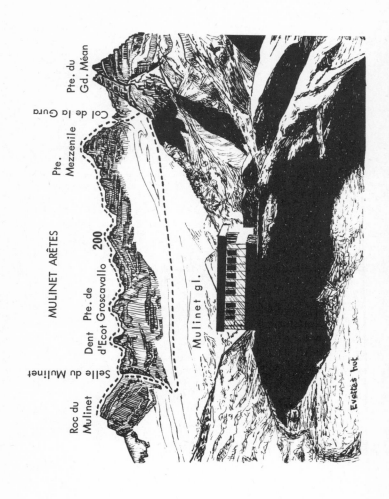

Roc du Mulinet

Selle du Mulinet

Dent Pte. de
d'Ecot Groscavallo

MULINET ARÊTES

200

Pte.
Mezzenile

Col de la Gura

Pte. du
Gd. Méan

Mulinet gl.

Evettes huť

from the Selle du Mulinet after taking the S-N way can be delicate in the afternoon; its couloir can be quite awkward compared with the Col Gura at the other end of the ridge. However the traverse is normally made from S to N and is described in this direction.

200 Mulinet Traverse. Axe and crampons should be taken. Examine ridge with glasses from a vantage pt. 50m N of hut to ascertain probable conditions. A competent party should allow 12h for round trip. AD, numerous pitches of III, some of III+/IV. Snow and ice on the many ledge traverses increases the difficulty. M. Bouvier with J.J. Blanc, 30 August 1895. P. Charles, K.D. Rice, 1973.

From the Evettes hut (R.94) descend the new path SSE down to the Reculaz gorge bridge (2499m). Contour edge of the Evettes plain S, then gradually work up moraines SE, crossing the stream issuing from the Gd. Méan gl. Follow moraine slopes on R (S) side of the stream to lower edge of gl. below the Pte. de Bonneval. Ascend alongside the moraine and slab-banks and bear NNE to cross the gl. (crevasses in the same direction) to reach on the far side the Col du Gd. Méan (3214m), which gives access to the Mulinet gl. further N (2¾h). From this col climb a steep snow slope E, forming the S edge of the Mulinet gl. The Col de la Gura 3362m) opens as 2 gaps in the frontier ridge at the top of this slope. Go to the L-hand gap by a steep but short snow/ice bit and a few rocks (15min., 3h from hut).

The ridge traverse commences here. From the N gap, pass through a notch on to the Ital. flank where several slabby steps slant up R to a chimney; the lower part is open while the upper part narrows to a slit giving a chockstone squeeze pitch (III). Exit L by easy rocks leading in loose steps back to crest which is taken steeply on slabs to Punta Mezzenile (3436m) (45min.). The ridge ahead drops vertically. Go down on the Fr. (W) side (III/III+, optional abseil) and when convenient traverse a ledge line to base of vertical step to rejoin the ridge. Follow pleasant crest over small towers (pitches of III/IV) to top of the last one (3377m), higher and steeper than the others. A short distance back, an easy chimney on the W side leads down to a traverse across the face to rejoin the ridge at the foot (3356m) of the next big tower. Climb the fine crest (pitches of III) to the Pte. de Groscavallo (3404m). Continue down the somewhat loose crest to the Selle de Groscavallo. From the gap climb a bank of slabs (III+) to finish up a zone of large loose blocks mingled with snow (delicate); pick the easiest way up the broad ridge to the Dent d'Ecot (3398m). From here descend the ESE (Ital.) ridge, not the main frontier ridge. Follow this over large blocks until a traverse N can be made into the upper part of a couloir filled with blocks and earth. Cross the couloir and rejoin the main ridge beyond; descend it to top of a steep step. Go down

125

FRANCESETTI
R.201

G F E D C B A

Mulinet gl.

Gd. Méan gl.

H

Evettes gl.

A Col de Bonneval R.203

B Pte. de Bonneval R.202

C Col du Grand Méan R.200

D Pte. Mezzenile R.200

E Roc du Mulinet R.200

F Levanna Orientale R.199

G Levanna Centrale R.198

H Bad moraine section beside
   lower icefall on R.203

the W flank and contour the step at a fairly low level, crossing broken ledges covered with large blocks. The level of the final part of this traverse is just below that of the Selle du Mulinet, which is reached without difficulty. The crest of the step may also be descended on good rock (III+). From the saddle climb the ridge in slabby steps to the top of the Roc du Mulinet.

Descent: Return to the Mulinet saddle and descend couloir on W side, at first by sound and easy rocks on the R side. About halfway down, cross to the L side and descend snow/ice. The rocks on this side become harder but they can be climbed or descended (III/III+). The bergschrund may be impassible in descent, but it is not difficult to arrange an abseil. At the foot of the couloir contour the upper slopes of the Mulinet gl., heading S towards the Col du Gd. Méan; a few large crevasses lie in the same direction. So rejoin the approach route; $3\frac{1}{2}$ h from Mulinet saddle back to hut; $5\frac{1}{2}$ h for ridge itself.

POINTE FRANCESETTI   3425m   3410m IGM

201   3633E. Culminating snow cap above the Gd. Méan gl., recommended local viewpoint and the most frequented gl. summit from the Evettes hut (R.94). F. First recorded ascent: W.A.B. Coolidge with C. Almer father & son, 21 July 1884. As for R.200 to the central plateau of the Gd. Méan gl. Cross the flat gl. to the foot of the W spur. The lower part is usually a rock slope then snow on the L of a supporting rockband running up to the summit; go up this slope to the top. Alternatively, turn up below spur on its S side in a gl. bay reaching up to the frontier ridge at the Col de la Disgrâce (3225m). From here climb SW side of mountain by a moderately steep couloir slope, part snow, part rock, to finish on a short summit ridge (either way to summit, $3\frac{1}{2}$–4h from hut).

POINTE DE BONNEVAL   3320m   3325m IGM

202   3633E. 100m error in all heights given along ridge by IGN; on current 1985 map, misprints 2 instead of 3 (eg. 3220 instead of 3320). Secondary barrier summit with several higher pts. than its principal measured projection; below this is the locally reputed NW pillar with an initial 200m of IV+/V on fairly sound rock.

POINTE DE SÉA   3213m   3217m IGM

POINTE TONINI   3327m   3324m IGM

203   3633E. <u>Traverse South-North.</u> F, with pitches of II. G. Corrà, L. Vaccarone with M. Rapelli, 24 August 1887. An excellent training

EVETTES GL. BASIN

A Grande Ciamarella 3676m
B Petite Ciamarella 3540m R.204
C Col Tonini 3244m R.203,205,206
D Col de la Petite Ciamarella 3433m
E Col W de la Ciamarella 3433m
G Italian usual route (snow covered shale)
H Pt. 3491
K Ridge junction pt. 3489

M Pt. 3534 R.205
N Pte. de Chalanson 3465m
P Pte. Tonini 3327m R.203
R Pte. Bonneval pt. 3256
S Pas de Chalanson 3310m
T Muraille d'Italie
V Tarn 2539m
X Evettes plain
Z Bad moraine section on R.203

route, providing a bit of everything. From the Evettes hut (R.94) descend the new path SSE to the Reculaz gorge bridge (2499m). Contour the edge of the Evettes plain S, soon crossing a rocky part covered with firm stones. A tarn is passed on the L, then skirt the base of an outcrop. Ahead is an icefall extending right across the Evettes gl. Take to the ice and climb a steeply crevassed section either by a gangway on the extreme L (climb its R side); or, 150m below the icefall traverse off the gl. to L and climb moraine and rounded rocks on the gl. bank, working L then R, somewhat loose and unpleasant. Above, continue SE across the upper gl. plateau below the Pte. de Séa and Tonini, avoiding several large crevasses cutting right across the slope. The final steepening to Col Tonini (3244m) is straightforward; small bergschrund and a short, narrow couloir of rocks and snow ($2\frac{3}{4}$ h).

Follow N a broad snow/scree ridge to Pte. Tonini. The summit tower is reached from the R as one approaches it (30 min.). Descend tower as it was climbed from the E, then traverse back L (NW) to the ridge running down to the Col de Séa. Stay on W side of crest, dropping down some 60m at one place to avoid a step. Below this return to the crest and cross to the E side. An easy slope leads to the col (3094m) (30 min.). The ridge ahead is tackled by an opening in the rocks just a short distance R of crest. Climb the steep break, moving R when in doubt, by a variety of pitches on good rock. Reach the narrow, exposed crest above its final plunge, about halfway to the Pte. de Séa summit. Follow crest as far as possible to the top; many variations (45 min.). From this summit descend a chimney on the E side and so turn the twin thumbs on the first part of the ridge going down to the Col de Bonneval (3152m). Return to the ridge and follow crest as closely as possible; turn small obstacles on the E side; pleasant, interesting work (30 min.).

From the col descend the W side by a slope of detestable scree and boulders, very steep, in which traces of a path are constantly shifting. Continue to the bottom where snow patches lead down to the Evettes gl. at the top of the icefall (30 min.). It is best to regain the lower part of the gl. by the variant on the E bank, via moraine, scree and slabby banks; the best route is not easy to find from above. So follow the outward leg back to the hut ($1\frac{1}{2}$ h, $7\frac{1}{4}$ h for round trip).

PETITE CIAMARELLA   3537m   3540m IGM

204   3633E. Height missing from 1985 printing of this map. C. Rabot with J. Blanc, G. Brun, 2 September 1878. Mistaken 1st British ascent claims date back to the 1890s, including Coolidge; probably not climbed by a British party until the 1930s. The NW face is the Evettes gl. headwall. Various good snow/ice climbs for early to mid season, 500m, AD/AD+.

GRANDE CIAMARELLA

Col E

R.205

3334

W ridge

R.206

Tonini gl.

3633E. One of the most impressive mountains in the Central Graian
Alps, tent-shaped, completely alpine and aloof on the N side, but a
walk-up on flaky schist/shale from the S in a dry season. It lies on a
spur detached entirely into Italy from pt.3489 on the frontier ridge,
near the Col W de la Ciamarella (3433m). Extensive summit panorama.
A. Tonini with G. Ambrosini, 31 July 1857. G. Yeld with J.J. Blanc,
A. Payot, 5 August 1878.

205   Normal French Route. A serious mixed climb, increasingly complicated by gl. recession and the exposure of decomposing rock. PD+/
AD. From the Evettes hut (R.94), as for R.203 to Col Tonini (3244m)
($2\frac{3}{4}$h). On the Ital. side cross the gl. basin, maintaining height if possible, and head directly towards the N face where it is lowest at its R
(W) end. The lowest dip is the so-called Col E de la Ciamarella at an
estimated 3440m. The face here is a mixture of horizontally layered
rocks covered with snow and ice, about 180m high and 45° steep. A
narrow band of snow/ice penetrates the barrier for some distance. Cross
the bergschrund, sometimes quite difficult, and climb the band as far
as possible; an alternative is steeper and very loose rock on either side.
Good frozen snow on the rock helps. Follow this line somewhat L of the
'col', up to the W ridge ($1\frac{3}{4}$h). At first the ridge is narrow, snow and
rock; cornice possible and delicate in most conditions. Follow crest
and climb first a long, low gendarme (3534m), called by the Italians,
the St. Robert rocks; this part can be avoided R (S) along a shelving
crescent snow ledge. Then climb or turn L (N) a second smaller version of the gendarme, after which the ridge broadens to an easy slope
and the summit in shale (1h, $5\frac{1}{2}$h from Evettes hut).

Descend the same route. An alternative is to go down the much easier
normal Ital. route, cut W across the Ciamarella gl. to the Pian Gias
gl., and ascend latter to re-enter France at the so-called Upper Chalanson pass, a snow brow at c.3375m just below the Selle de l'Albaron.
This still leaves a descent of the entire Evettes gl. F+ (6h back to hut).

206   North Face. A popular snow/ice climb, normally taken in a line
somewhat R of the summit, between 2 groups of rock in the lower half
of the face. 400m, angle in upper part 50-52° for a short distance,
AD+/D, very variable. E. Ferreri, M. Walter-Levi, 4 June 1922.
W. Cheverst, J. Kitchen, 1972. As for R.205 to foot of face ($3\frac{1}{4}$h).
Cross the difficult bergschrund and climb the snow/ice face a short
way R of rocks exposed below the hanging sérac across the upper part
of the face. Keep R of summit line until above the steepest part, at the
sérac level, then trend L directly towards the summit (4-5h from foot
of face). The face has been climbed L of the sérac line.

ALBARON

Selle

SE ridge R.207

Evettes gl.

ALBARON

Selle de l'Albaron

207

Col du Greffier

PIC REGAUD

208

208

Evettes gl.

207

Allard CR

ALBARON 3637m

3633E. A worthy pendant to the Ciamarella, projecting as a spur into France from the frontier ridge at the Selle de l'Albaron. Essentially a gl. peak; all sides are covered by a variety of gl. terrain, and crevasse/sérac obstacles predominate. R.C. Nichols with J.V. Favret, 2 September 1866.

207 South-East Ridge. The normal route, attained from the Evettes and Avérole huts, and from the Ital. Gastaldi hut, with little difficulty, all F/F+, but serious gl. work. Only the Evettes approach is given here; it is certainly the most beautiful; the crevasses and bergschrunds are complex in arrangement and vary from year to year.

As for R.203 to top of the first icefall (1¾h). Now head S across the middle gl. plateau to the highest inlet below the lowest pt. in the head wall – Pas de Chalanson (3310m). Bear R (W) among crevasses and a rupture, keeping L to avoid ice walls and long slits. Go up an obvious gl. ramp NW into a snow/ice scoop skirting the rocks called Muraille d'Italie. Then bear L (S) round another group of big crevasses and so reach the final slopes with fewer crevasses leading to the Selle de l' Albaron (3474m) at foot of the SE ridge (2½h). Climb a short steep snow dome to a stretch of broad ridge, narrowing to a rocky section, along which small steps are turned on R side. A narrow snow ridge of moderate angle follows, cornice possible. A further short stepped rock crest leads to a false summit. Walk along a broad snowfield to the main top at the far N end (1h, 5¼h from Evettes hut).

PIC REGAUD 3232m

3633E. Conspicuous rock peak on W side of Evettes cirque. The rock is a greenish smooth serpentine, good when it is steep and clean as in an abundance of fine slabs, but otherwise loose. Stonefall danger and prone to verglas in damp conditions. The classic route is the N ridge, AD with pitches of III/III+/IV (A. Chambre with A. & P. Blanc, 1922). The ordinary route is tricky to find in descent. J. Mathieu, C. Regaud with J.J. & J.M. Blanc, 17 July 1895. C.F. Meade with P. Blanc, 6 August 1911.

208 South-East Flank. PD with short bits of II. Care needed with loose rock. From the Evettes hut (R.94) return along the path to the Col des Evettes for 5min. then cut off L down a narrow track which in another 5 min. disappears temporarily in a small grassy plain, to reappear in 150m under a prominent square boulder. Follow track above W side of Evettes gl. moraines until a cairn and stone with paint mark is reached at a corner in the track. (There are other cairns, before and after the correct one). Here ascend R on a steep grassy rib towards the

135

peak. Follow rib until it vanishes into stones. Continue in the same line, across stones and boulders among grass patches, keeping R when in doubt. Follow this line to the highest grass tongue, which abuts an indefinite rocky rib. (There is a more conspicuous and parallel rib to the L again, which forms the skyline). Climb the steep rib to a cairn at its top – unpleasant, between large loose blocks. Here commences the traverse line below the E face of the mountain, well seen from the hut. Follow it S along an undulating terrace where brown rock meets the black face of the mountain above, first across scree and earth to a perched boulder. Just beyond it, climb steep broken rocks, light red in colour, delicate (10m, II), and continue up to the L over scree to highest part of the terrace. Follow terrace as close to the wall of the mountain as possible; some stonefall danger for 10 min. After a descent the terrace finally rises to snow at the edge of the Evettes gl. upper terrace, a short way below the Col du Greffier (3086m) (2¼ h).

There are variable ways to go up the SE flank, but the longest, by the col, is the safest as regards stonefall. Follow the loose edge of the gl. slope to more rubble leading to the col. Now cross a broken rocky slope R and enter a big gully which is taken to just below the S ridge. Exit R along a ledge system to gain the top of a secondary ridge plunging below. From here go up diagonally R along a system of narrow ledges to enter another large gully. Climb its R side to the S ridge and scramble this pleasantly to summit (2 h, 4¼ h from Evettes hut).

BESSANESE 3592m 3604m IGM

3634E. These heights refer to Signal Tonini (see below). Bold rock peak with a local reputation not entirely deserved. The Italian (E) face is 600m high and has several comparatively easy routes on variable rock; serious undertakings; the Gastaldi hut (2659m) is finely situated below this face. The Avérole hut serves the more laborious Fr. approaches. The N ridge from the Col de la Bessanese is a long classic rock climb. The summit ridge is adorned by 3 towers: N to S, Signal Rey (c.3595m), Signal Baretti (c.3620m), Signal Tonini (3592/3604m). First ascents: Tonini – A. Tonini with a local man, 31 August 1857. Baretti – M. Baretti with G. Cibrario, 26 July 1873; W.A.B. Coolidge with C. Almer father & son, 27 July 1883. Rey – G. Rey with A. Castagneri, 2 September 1889 (1st ascent of N ridge); C.F. Meade with J.J. & P. Blanc, 21 August 1901.

209 South Flank. Normal Fr. route, tedious approach with a welcome scramble to finish. PD, with one pitch of II+, good rock. From the Avérole hut (R.95) follow path SE traversing grassy slopes, crossing the Veilet stream and approaching the Arnès torrent, coming down a narrow defile from the gl. The path goes steeply through the gorge

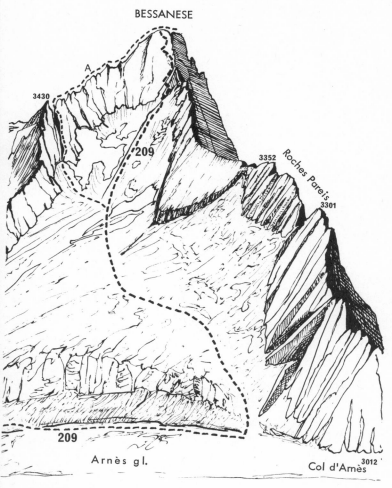

BESSANESE

A

3430

209

3352

Roches Pareis

3301

Arnès gl.

209

Col d'Arnès 3012

A = SW ridge var. (III+)

in a corridor of large blocks on the L side. Emerge on a narrow plain and head towards the gl. Avoid the lower ice tongue by keeping L on loose moraine, midway between the bed and the cliff which flanks the approach. A little higher it may be better to walk on the ice (crevasses); go up to within 200m of the foot of the Pte. d'Arnès SW face, where cliffs on the L relent. Ascend diagonally NW over banks of steep loose moraine. Continue this line to a moraine wilderness – stones and snowbeds. Take a fairly low line, well away from the parallel Roches Pareis. Turn up gradually into steep moraine cwm (snowfield) below the SSW facet of mountain. For the final steep ascent of cwm, traces of a path can be found in the R side lateral moraine, high up, approaching the upper part of the Roches Pareis ridge. From the top of this moraine go up to a couloir on R, coming from a gap between the Roches and Bessanese proper. Reach an obvious ledge break about 60m above its R side by crossing scree, snow and ledges in a movement L. From the last ledge on a corner overlooking the couloir climb a series of walls straight up (II-) to a break below a further steepness. Now traverse L to gully bed and climb loose rock on its L side; the upper part is steep and can be icy. Emerge on a short snow/ice edge in the gap, which abuts the final buttress ($4\frac{1}{2}$ h).

The face above is guarded by a wall, then slabs tilting L. From the knife edge either descend 8m on E side to a fine ledge and 3m along this climb a near vertical pitch (15m, III-) to land on a glacis at the bottom R-hand end of the slabs. Or, it is better to step off the knife edge and climb vertical rocks for 3m, then go up a gangway L for 6m, and return R on excellent holds in an exposed situation (II+). The L edge of the slabby zone is the crest. Follow it pleasantly until the ridge steepens. Steeper rocks for a few m, then a staircase trending R, to finish after 90m at Signal Tonini (45 min., $5\frac{1}{4}$ h from hut).

To reach the higher Signal Baretti, descend ridge to gap between the 2 towers. Contour Baretti on the W side by a narrow sloping terrace, snow covered as a rule, often icy and delicate, and with a void below it. At the far end step into the gap just behind Baretti and reach its summit by the main (N) ridge (15 min. from Tonini). Or, about half way along the sloping terrace, a chimney in the face of the tower, just R of the summit, can be climbed on excellent rock, steep and strenuous (III+).

OUILLE D'ARBÉRON   3563m   3560m IGM

3634E. Punta d'Arnàs. An easy mountain and fine regional viewpoint, well worth a visit. A large cairn marks the lower SE end of the summit ridge (3554m). L. Barale with A, B. & G. Castagneri, 14 July 1873. W.A.B. Coolidge with C. Almer father & son, 26 July 1883.

BESSANESE summit towers

Rey

Baretti

l'edgebant

Tonini

CROIX ROUSSE

3541

3457

3427 R.211

Col Martelli

Baounet gl.

210 Traverse by West-South-West and South-South-East Ridges. An easy combination, recommended, F to main top. The crest to pt.3554 is PD-, the descent, F. From the Avérole hut (R.95) as for R.209 to head of the corridor/gorge, a few min. after the Arnès gl. comes into sight (1¼ h). Turn sharp R (S), cross stream and work up over and round 2 large grass and slab-rock hummocks (2722m) into a barren cwm on the NE side of the Ouille de la Vallettaz. The general direction is SSE. Go high round a moraine lake (2914m) on the E side, then work straight up the frontal moraines to the vicinity of the Col d'Arbéron (3045m) (1¼ h). Climb L-wards (E) across rockbands on the edge overlooking the Arbéron gl., coming down as a plain snow/ice slope between the NW and WSW ridges. Go up easy rocks to the E to reach the side of the gl. , then cross the gl. slightly upwards to reach the WSW ridge almost anywhere (45 min.). Go up ridge to summit, broad and stony, keeping near crest or just below it on R side, traces of a path (45 min.). Beyond, the summit rock crest is narrow and very exposed on the L. Climb or turn small towers by their R side to reach large cairn at the far end (15 min., 4¼ h from Avérole hut).

Descend the rocky SSE crest, sometimes snowy, to Col Martelli (3269m) (30 min.). Step down a few rocks to the head of the almost level N bay of the Baounet gl. and descend it close to the R side, avoiding several large open crevasses. After 15 min. go on to rocks on the R side and contour rough but easy ground to the W and NW, round the broad base of the WSW ridge. Recross the base of the Arbéron gl. and rejoin the approach route. Alternatively, descend from the N bay to the main part of the Baounet gl. and climb the SW side of the Col d'Arbéron below the Ouille de la Vallettaz (2¾ h, 3¼ h from summit back to hut, 7½ h for round trip).

CROIX ROUSSE 3571m 3566m IGM

3634E. Croce Rossa. Very similar sort of summit to the Ouille d'Arbéron, with which it can be combined to make a not unduly long traverse of ample interest. The main survey top (3541m) is at the head of the WSW spur. A. Tonini and a local man, July 1857. W.A.B. Coolidge with C. Almer father & son, 26 July 1883.

211 Traverse by North and South Ridges. A mixed climb, PD- for a short way above Col Martelli, otherwise, F. It is shorter to descend the WSW spur, if desired. As for R.210 to the Col d'Arbéron; now down steep scree/snow on its S side to the Baounet gl. Ascend the gl. close round the S flank of the Ouille d'Arbéron, up into the N gl.bay. Reach Col Martelli (3269m) directly ahead, avoiding several large crevasses (4 h). The col overlooks the huge Rossa lake. Now climb the snow/rock crest to a step. Turn this on R (W) side by a long broken

gutter, rejoining crest near an obvious shoulder (3427m). Continue by the sharp crest, or descend slightly to the gl. slopes on E side and cross them keeping L of crest to reach the W top; now curve round easily E to the E top (1¼ h, 5¼ h from Avérole hut).

Follow rocky crest S down to the Col de la Valette (3212m). A short rock step can be taken direct, or turned R (45 min.). From col return along the almost flat Baounet gl. to rejoin the outward route (3 h, 3¾ h from summit back to hut; 9 h for round trip).

POINTE DE CHARBONNEL   3752m

3634E. Mighty mountain standing in isolation between the frontier ridge and the Arc valley. Although situated directly opposite the Avérole hut, none of the ways from here can be recommended. Consequently rarely climbed, as the only alpine route is long; however, it is most worthwhile, especially in good conditions and starting from a bivouac. Splendid regional panorama. M.A. Boniface, M.A. Fodéré, J. & M. Personnaz, 17 July 1862. W.A.B. Coolidge with C. Almer father & son, 10 July 1876.

212 Morth-West Side (Charbonnel Glacier). Fine gl. climb, rather spoiled by long, continuously steep approach and with possible enhanced difficulty caused by gl. recession. PD/PD+. Start from the road in the Avérole valley (R.31, 95), just below Vincendières hamlet, at the br. near pt. 1830; campsite one km towards Bessans. Cross river and join downstream the much improved (by electricity board) zigzag path rising steeply SW up the grassy spur between the Chenaillon and Charbonnel streams. Go up at length until at the top the path zags R (W). Break off L and follow traces with a few cairns SE through the lowest slanting rockbands, to make a rising traverse in this direction to cross the infant Charbonnel torrent. Climb its bed on L side then bear away L between 2 rockbands, along a stony terrace system. Here at c.2800m (below pt.2930), reasonable biv. sites (2¾ h). Continue SE up broken terraces and rock steps, sometimes snowy, to reach a fairly obvious break in the slanting rockbands under N edge of the gl. Go up this break to the gl. at pt.3208; verglassed slabs due to watermelt is a common condition - tricky; similarly, getting established on the gl. can involve an ice slope, crossed by a rising traverse R. Ascend gl. in same SE direction, keeping a little L of the summit line, at a steady angle approaching 40° with crevasses possible anywhere. Cross bergschrund at L end and trend R to E end of the summit ridge (3-4 h, 5¾-6¾ h from road). Comfortable descent in good conditions to road in 3 h.

POINTE DE RONCE 3612m

3634E, 3634W. Punta Roncia. This great mountain towers above the Mont Cenis lake and pass, while the NW flank overlooks the Arc valley. Like the Charbonnel, only the NW side offers an alpine route. Magnificent summit panorama. R. De Lamanon, an English traveller, and one other, with a hunter called Bouvier, 15 July 1784. Hunters had been to the summit previously. W.A.B. Coolidge with C. Almer father & son, 14 July 1884.

213 <u>North-West Side</u>. Pleasant gl. expedition, PD. B. & J. Leclerc, 15 August 1925. R.G. Collomb, R.S. Mowll, 4 August 1965. From the Arcelle Neuve ch. (2203m), R.97, follow the path S round a bend (2236m) to the Arcelle Neuve stream. Ascend grassy slopes on its L (N) side, bearing away to mount steadily E toward an obvious rock bandstand called the Cailla (3010m). Follow a rib L to mount flat debris terraces just L (N) of this pt. Go up debris S, skirting the inner L side of the bandstand, to move L onto large gl. snowfield under the N side of the double headed Signal du Gd. Mt. Cenis. Make a rising traverse L over snowfield (crevasses possible) to cut through a few rock outcrops at E side, just below pt.3234. Now bear up S on the main Arcelle Neuve gl., crevassed, with one section at 40°, and a bergschrund, to skirt the top of the N gl. spur, under the little rocky pt. 3584, and follow a nice snow edge SE to summit (4½h from the chalet).

ROCCIAMELONE 3538m

214 3634E. Fr. Rochemelon. The ascent of this mountain by Rotario d'Asti on 1 September 1358 confers upon it a unique place in Alpine history. The event is celebrated today by an annual religious fête and pilgrimage to the summit – now adorned with a chapel and various statues. The upper part of the mountain is situated entirely in Italy. The shortest route from France follows the entire length of the long and straight Ribon valley, starting near Bessans. Severe gl. recession has forced the approach on to the Rochemelon gl. first to ascend rocky terraces on the N side of the snout. The route is marked fairly accurately on the map. From Bessans to summit, 7h, or from the Arcelle ch. (R.96), 4½h. In Italy, above the small town of Susa (501m), it is possible to drive a car to the Riposa roadhead (2205m), then a big easy path in grass to the Ca'd'Asti hut (2854m) (1½h); from here by a good path eventually in rocks on the SSW ridge to the summit (1¾h, 3¼h from roadhead).

Index